# LEARNING TO LEAN

*Books by Marion B. West*

LEARNING TO LEAN
TWO OF EVERYTHING BUT ME
NO TURNING BACK
OUT OF MY BONDAGE

# Learning to Lean ___

## Marion B. West

A DOUBLEDAY-GALILEE ORIGINAL
Doubleday & Company, Inc., Garden City, New York  1980

Library of Congress Cataloging in Publication Data

West, Marion B
    Learning to lean.

    "A Doubleday-Galilee original."
    1. Christian life—1960–     2. West, Marion B.
I. Title.
BV4501.2.W4345     248'.4
ISBN: 0-385-15088-1
Library of Congress Catalog Card Number 79–7514

# CONTENTS

# INTRODUCTION

A few years ago someone said to me with open impatience, "All religion is a crutch! Who needs it?"

I didn't say anything, but in my mind I saw a pair of crutches and thought, "But crutches aren't a good thing. We should walk straight and tall, secure and alone."

I tried to do just that for years. In the process I found that being a wife and mother wasn't at all like what I thought it would be. In desperation, I came to the place that I could hardly crawl, and at times I felt like not even moving or trying to walk again. It was during this period of despair that I made a discovery that still amazes me.

God intended His only son, Jesus Christ—not religion—to be a crutch for all who need to lean. So I began leaning—cautiously at first—then heavily, securely on Him. I leaned in all sorts of situations. Big ones, little ones, scary ones, even funny ones. Leaning was wonderful!

But even now a crafty, silent voice urges, "Try it on your own. You don't really need to lean anymore." And so I try and inevitably I find that I must once again lean on Him. He welcomes me. No longer in my mind do I picture crutches.

But I see instead the Cross of Calvary, beautiful and horrible, that makes possible the daily miracle of leaning on Jesus.

Learning to lean seems to be a lifetime process.

August 10, 1977
Lilburn, Georgia

". . . yet will they lean upon the Lord, and say, Is not the Lord among us? none evil can come upon us." (Micah 3:11, KJV)

"Trust in the Lord with all thine heart; and lean not unto thine own understanding. In all thy ways acknowledge him, and he shall direct thy paths." (Proverbs 3:5–6, KJV)

## LEARNING TO LEAN

I'm learning to lean, learning to lean,
Learning to lean on Jesus,
Finding more power than I'd ever dreamed,
I'm learning to lean on Jesus,
The joy I can't explain fills my soul
Since the day I made Jesus my King,
His blessed Holy Spirit is leading my way,
He's teaching and I'm learning to lean.
There's glorious victory each day now for me,
I've found His peace so serene.
He helps me with each task if only I'll ask,
Every day now, I'm learning to lean.
Learning to lean, learning to lean,
I'm learning to lean on Jesus.

# LEARNING TO LEAN

# I

## THE GENTLE TOUCH

Entering the familiar shopping mall, I suddenly wanted to turn around and go back home. Shopping was usually fun, especially when looking for a new dress, but not today.

I'd just learned that somehow the edited manuscript of my new book had been mistakenly thrown away at the publisher's. I had another exact copy, but the news had still devastated me. A manuscript becomes almost like a child, even mailing my first one had been traumatic. I couldn't seem to leave the post office. I kept hanging around, looking at my book manuscript stacked with other packages. I wanted to run tell the postmaster, "Please be gentle with it." Sending a manuscript off with strangers was almost identical to sending a child off to camp for the first time.

I tried to be grateful that I had a copy of the book, but no matter how hard I tried, gloom settled around me and I didn't really care about a new dress. I'd just gotten the copy of the manuscript off in the mail (after xeroxing a copy for myself). Coming out of the post office, deep in thought, I pulled right out in front of a car. The driver slammed on the brakes and blew his horn long and loud at me. I was grateful I couldn't hear what he was saying. Even when I apologized, his anger didn't vanish. Everyone glared at me. By the time I entered the shopping center, I was near tears. "Ridiculous," I told myself. "You've never gotten a parking ticket or had a fender bender. Pulling out in front of a car is no big deal. It's wonderful that an accident didn't occur.

"And the new manuscript will be there soon. Nothing will happen to it," I reasoned with myself, "buck up. You're fine. You can handle this. The contract's already been signed."

A nasty, silent voice suggested, "Bet the cover of the book won't be good. It'll be without feeling. You know how picky you are about covers. This book's just doomed."

I knew the voice. The father of lies, the accuser. The one who plants seeds of doubt and loves to suggest, "What if . . ."

I'd been trying to battle him again, on my own, and he was winning. He knew it, and I did too. A tear slid down my face as I stood looking in at store mannequins. They all looked so happy and carefree. They had small waists too, I noticed, looking down at my own. It used to be a size 22, I thought sadly. "Get hold of yourself. People will stare at you if you stand here and cry." Wiping the lone tear away, I walked into the store briskly, hoping I looked happy and a little carefree like the store mannequins.

Inside the store I began looking through the dresses without enthusiasm. It was one of the nicest stores in the mall. I'd already decided no budget shops today. I wanted something really spiffy.

Suddenly I became aware of a woman humming very softly. I almost recognized the tune. Then she stopped. I didn't look up. I kept my eyes on the dress in my hand, but my heart had leaped. "Father," I prayed silently, "please let her hum again, that same melody." I wasn't sure what it was, just a few more lines, and I could identify it.

"Hummm-mmmmm-mmmmmmmmm," came the sweet sounds once again. Relieved, I felt myself smile and acknowledged the new spark of joy in my heart. I didn't feel alone anymore. I thought about the words: "Shackled by a heavy burden, 'neath a load of guilt and shame. Then the hand of Jesus touched me and now I am no longer the same. He touched me! He touched me! And oh, the joy that floods my soul. Something happened and now I know, He touched me and made me whole."*

I looked into the radiant face of the woman who managed the shop. She hadn't noticed me yet. I asked without a moment's hesitation, "Has He touched you?" I couldn't believe I spoke the words so easily. Would she even know what I was talking about?

She looked at me, smiled—her face positively glowed. Then she clapped her hands together in a silent gesture and said softly, "Oh, yes! He's touched me." She looked at me more intently and asked, "He's touched you too, hasn't He?"

I nodded.

---

"How long have you been a Christian?" I asked eagerly.

"Nearly twenty years." She was probably in her fifties.

Suddenly I was pouring out my deep, private feelings to her. There seemed to be no way I could stop the flow of words. Very unlike me. I usually listen to other people's troubles, preferring to keep mine to myself, sharing them only with the Lord. Besides, she was working. She appeared to be there just for me, though. She kept smiling as I told her about my book. She smiled like the problem was no bigger than a gnat. Then right there in the middle of that plush dress shop, she raised her hands slightly and prayed for my book on its way to the publishers. She told Satan that he couldn't touch it anymore. She prayed for the cover too. She went on to pray for me and my family. She thanked Jesus for shedding His blood for me and my problems. When we opened our eyes, I didn't have a troubled heart anymore. The problem had vanished. I felt tempted to look around the store for it. But I knew it was gone. It had been gobbled up by her simple prayer. I felt God's presence in a mighty way. I didn't know whether to laugh or cry. God still cared about me . . . and about my book.

"Now," she asked, "what kind of dress do you want?"

I was excited about my dress now, and my new friend, Cora Cummings. I tried on a bright green number with a matching scarf. Unusual for me. I usually stick with brown and tans. But not today. When I came out of the dressing room, Cora and another saleslady smiled and nodded. I overheard the other woman's comment: "She has a nice, small waist for that dress."

Miracle of miracles! Maybe I wasn't getting a thick middle after all. When I took the dress off, I noticed it was a size seven. I usually wear a ten, but today a seven fit. I accepted it without question, just as I accepted Cora's friendship and prayer.

The book was released months later, and when I saw the cover for the first time, I cried. There was warmth and feeling in it and even soft browns. A few other problems that the publisher said we might encounter weren't there. A space problem had been solved. A national inspirational magazine excerpted the book, and it seemed to be well received. Through all of this I thought back to Cora's powerful prayer and how the Lord arranged for us to meet. Almost every time I wear the green dress I think of Cora. She's become one of my dearest friends.

Ours was a gentle meeting that we could so easily have missed. She could have refused to hum when the Lord suggested it to her, or I could have refused to speak to her because of pride. But my loving Father reached out and reminded me through Cora, "Lean, Marion, lean on Me again."

# 2

## THE ANONYMOUS CALLER

I hurried to answer the ringing phone. Even though I was busy and didn't have time to talk, I hoped my "Hello" sounded cheerful enough.

Silence.

"Hello." A little louder.

Silence again. Then the caller hung up.

I hung up too. Probably a wrong number. Yet, I didn't walk away. For some reason, I stood by the phone, half-expecting it to ring again.

It rang instantly, and this time a young girl, probably in her early teens, said something lewd and hung up with a loud bang.

I answered the phone six more times. Each time there was only silence, except for once. The caller laughed and spoke, using a filthy word in a sentence about me.

The normal thing to do would be not to answer the phone again. Or simply take it off the hook and leave it for a while. I was busy, and I didn't want to listen to the insults and filth.

The phone shrilled again. I had to decide whether to answer it or not. "Don't answer it," came the thought. "Don't subject yourself to that anymore. Enough is enough."

Another voice, very patient and soft, suggested, "That girl is about the age of the girls that you teach in Sunday school. I'll help you. Answer it," the Silent Voice urged.

Even as I raced for the phone, I prayed, "Oh, Lord, can't we just ignore her?"

"That's what everyone that she's called has been doing."

I made my decision quickly and, taking a deep breath, said, "Hello," once again as I prayed, "Help me, Lord." I was amazed to find that this time my heart had stopped hammering and there was a new calmness in my voice as though I expected to speak to an old friend.

Silence.

"Hello," I said again softly. "Would you like to talk to me about something. I'll listen."

Silence. But she didn't hang up.

Then without warning she spit out another four-letter word and seemed to wait for my reaction.

I began praying out loud, "Dear Jesus, please show this confused child that You love her, care deeply about her and want to change her. Help her realize that You died for her personally, and she doesn't have to do things like this." As I prayed, a thought crossed my mind, "She's going to hang up on you. Why don't you hang up on her first? Stop this foolish prayer for an obscene caller."

I felt a little ridiculous, but kept praying, "Lord, help her understand somehow that I love her too, but You love her so much more. Help her know I forgive her for what she's doing and that You will too, if she'll ask. You can show what real joy and thrills are. Lord, she doesn't understand about Your unconditional love. Please teach her some way. Make her what You want her to be."

I could actually feel the caller listening, and I believed that she would continue to listen as long as I prayed. But I ended my prayer. After the amen followed silence.

"Do you want to talk?" I asked.

She hung up, but gently this time.

I waited, and the phone rang again.

Suddenly I had an idea. "Jennifer," I called to my fourteen-year-old daughter, who'd been watching the whole episode, "find a 'Four Spiritual Laws'—quick."

The "Four Spiritual Laws" is a small booklet put out by Campus Crusade for Christ. By simply reading through it, in just a few moments anyone can explain to someone how to begin a new life in Christ. Scripture references and simple explanations make the Four Laws an easy tool to use.

While Jennifer searched through my purse, the phone rang again. "Hurry, Jen."

She handed me the booklet on the third ring.

"Hello," I said.

Silence.

"I'd like to share something with you." I began reading slowly in a soft voice that didn't even sound like mine: "God loves you and has a wonderful plan for your life." As I read the section that explains how sin separates each of us from God, the caller said curtly, "This isn't Sunday, Reverend."

"Jesus loves you every day," I said and continued reading. When I got to the part explaining how to invite Jesus into her heart, she interrupted, "I'm glad you can read, lady."

On my own I would have hung up on her. Smart-talking youngsters anger me when nothing else will. I felt only love for her, and replied, "And I'm so glad that you can listen."

When I got to the last page that told how each of us must individually invite Jesus into our hearts, I was once again interrupted. The young girl snapped, "There's a no-trespassing sign on my heart, lady!"

Her voice sounded different now, deeper. She could have been crying. She hung up, and the phone didn't sound again.

I began to pray for her and to expect her calls. Sometimes they came long after I was in bed. Sometimes she spoke, other times the silence. The obscene language stopped. She began to ask questions about my life and family. We talked more comfortably. Several times we laughed.

Months passed and I didn't hear from her, then she called late one evening. I'd been asleep and couldn't get my thoughts together. There was a note of joy about her voice. I was too sleepy to beat around the bush, so I mumbled half-awake, "Don't you want to invite Jesus into your heart and start going to church somewhere?"

I really woke up when she answered, "I am now a Christian. He's in my heart and I attend —— Church." I knew the church well. Then she told me her name and address. She lived in a lovely section not far from me. I called her by her name, and it was good to at last be able to address her personally. She told me about her church and Sunday school teacher, then said, "Well, I gotta go now. Thanks. Bye."

It was the first time she'd ever said bye to me. Even though we'd talked on a friendly basis for a while, she'd just hang up suddenly. The bye sounded nice. I liked it. I suspected it was our final goodbye, and it turned out to be. We've never talked again, and I've even forgotten her name and address. But she knows the Lord. Her name's written in the Lamb's Book, and now she'll never be anonymous to God.

*3* ——————————————————————————

## MY FIRST FRUIT
## (OF THE SPIRIT) CAKE

"Know what I want for Christmas, this year?" my husband asked as we sat in our den reading the newspaper.

Whatever it is, I thought, you're sure giving me plenty of time to get it. Christmas is almost two months away. "What?" I asked.

"I want you to bake a fruit cake—from scratch."

I dropped my paper and stared at him to see if his eyes told me he was teasing.

Nope. He was serious.

"You know I can't even make a decent biscuit."

"Well, that's what I want." He read the recipe section of the paper. "Look at this one." Jerry handed me the paper and pointed to "Grandma's Old Fashioned Fruit Cake." It called for things I'd never even heard of.

"I don't know what some of this stuff is," I wailed.

"They'll tell you at the store," he grinned.

He'll probably forget all about this, I decided. He'd talked about my baking cakes before. Surely, he doesn't really think I can bake a fruit cake that we can eat. I'd had to throw away cake pans that the cakes couldn't be scraped out of. Besides, I thought, cheerfully, his mother always makes us a cake at Christmas.

But for the next few weeks Jerry asked such questions as, "Have you thought any more about the fruit cake?" "Did you save the recipe section of the paper?" "When will you get started?"

Finally I hit upon an idea. I'd have a woman I knew who was an excellent cook make the cake for me. I'd pay her anything. Jerry would have his cake. I just wouldn't make it.

I told him that he would have the cake, carefully avoiding the truth.

"Great," he beamed. "I want to sit in the kitchen and talk to you while you make it. I want to watch you cut up the stuff and smell it cooking."

I fumed for days. I'd pull out the section of the paper with the recipe in it and stare at it. I suddenly felt like the girl in the fairy tale who was commanded to spin straw into gold.

Sitting on my stool in the kitchen, I studied the smiling face of a woman who'd baked a fruit cake. Good for you, I thought. But cooking is not my talent.

After a few more days, I started talking to the Lord about the problem. "Lord, You know I can't make cakes. That's not my thing. I could paint him a picture or write him a poem."

The Lord didn't seem to give me a nod of approval.

So I continued, "Anyway, Lord, Jerry wants me to enjoy baking this fruit cake. He wants me to hum and bustle around in the kitchen in my apron. Lord, I can't make the cake joyfully. I'd be ugly about making it. And if I did make it, it wouldn't come out of the pan, I'll bet."

The Lord seemed to answer with scripture: "I can do all things through Christ which strengtheneth me" (Philippians 4:13, KJV).

I sighed, "Okay, Lord, with Your help, I'll make Jerry this fruit cake. But first give me the desire to do it and a real joy about baking. I don't want to grumble and murmur. And please let it come out of the pan."

I told nearly everyone I saw the next day, "I'm baking Jerry a fruit cake for Christmas." People smiled, nodded. Some told me they'd already baked six. Nevertheless, I was still excited about my cake.

Visiting a neighbor the next day, the subject of baking fruit cakes came up. She told me about an excellent, never-fail recipe she'd used for years. She showed me the recipe. I made a copy and asked Jerry if it would be all right if I made that one instead of Grandma's.

He grinned and said, "Sure."

I knew what all the items were in this recipe. I wasn't overjoyed about the three pints of nuts that were required. But I shelled them, and discovered that shelling nuts is a real labor of love. One of our eight-year-old twins offered to help. I knew he'd make a mess and eat more than he shelled, but I smiled and said, "Okay."

Jeremy sat down and shelled for three hours. His brother, Jon, joined him. They turned out to be good help. I sat with them a lot, and we talked while we shelled the pecans. I felt sort of like John Boy Walton's mother.

Finally we had three pints of nuts. I put them in a large jar and placed them in the refrigerator with a label that read "Don't eat. For Daddy's fruit cake."

Gathering my items together for the cake later in the week, I realized that I really did have a peace about this cake—just like I'd baked for years. Finally the day came that I began. Jerry came in the kitchen and watched. The twins brought in some of their friends and announced proudly, "Our mother's baking a fruit cake." Our teen-aged daughters Julie, sixteen, and Jennifer, fourteen, came downstairs to watch with open enthusiasm. The kitchen was like a three-ring circus with so many spectators, but I didn't seem to mind, somehow. I didn't even want to scream, "Everybody out." I felt a new kindness for my family and even for the neighborhood children who watched.

Jerry commented several times about how good it was of me to bake him this cake, and I wondered why I hadn't done it sooner. We peeked in the oven together many times—sort of like people looking at television when it first came out in the fifties. And I had followed the directions this time—no guessing and no short cuts.

Just before time to take the cake out, I thought, "Why, this hasn't been hard at all." I had a very gentle feeling about the whole experience. Gone was my rebellion at being asked to bake a cake. I almost hated that the experience was over, except that the big moment was nearly at hand—turning my cake out of the pan.

After letting it cool according to directions, I turned it upside down very carefully. Nothing happened. I tapped on the pan. It didn't budge. My family gathered around for the big moment. I prayed silently, "Lord, I've come this far with Your help. I refuse to believe You won't help me get this cake out of the pan perfectly."

"It's coming," one of the twins screamed. And it did. It plopped onto the waiting plate and we all stared, almost in disbelief. Then slowly everyone's startled looks turned into enormous grins. My cake looked like something out of *Good Housekeeping*.

I packed it away in an air-tight plastic sack. One day just before Christmas, I cut a piece. Oh, it was delicious! I served it with joy at a Sunday school party, and women who've baked for years asked for my recipe. Jerry proudly asked friends over for "some of Marion's fruit cake."

It wasn't until after Christmas when reading my Bible one night that I lingered over a familiar passage that had a new meaning for me: "But when the Holy Spirit controls our lives he will produce this kind of fruit in us: love, joy, peace, patience, kindness, goodness, faithfulness, gentleness and self-control" (Galatians 5:22–23, TLB).

Then I suddenly realized that because I couldn't do it by myself and had asked for help, the Lord had taught me step-by-step how to make a fruit *of the Spirit* cake.

# 4

## THE BUTCHER AND ME

There are two kinds of women: those who can talk with butchers, and those who can't. The butcher can always tell the difference instantly.

I made this discovery when I was still a bride. Just married, and grocery shopping for the first time, I felt butterflies in my stomach as I approached the meat counter. It all looked alike to me. Other women selected their purchases quickly and confidently. I didn't know what to buy or how to cook it.

Greatly impressed with women who asked for special cuts of meat, I listened carefully, watching one lady in particular. She rang the buzzer confidently. A grim butcher appeared from behind swinging doors. As soon as he saw her, he smiled, "Good morning, Mrs. Morgan. What can I get for you?"

"Hello, Charles. I want a roast exactly like the one you cut for me last week; twelve pork chops, center cut, and four one-and-a-half-inch steaks." (Remember, this was twenty years ago.)

My mouth fell open. *Would he get all that for her, when he already had meat in the counter?*

"Be right back," he smiled.

I kept looking down at packages of ground beef, pretending I could see some difference in them.

The swinging doors parted again and the butcher held up the roast for her approval. To my disbelief, she refused it! Still smiling, he took it back and brought out another one which she accepted. "In time," I thought, "I'll be able to do that too."

The butcher glared at me, and I quickly threw a package of hamburger into my cart, smiled gratefully at him, and moved on.

Several months and many stores later my fear of butchers had grown. I watched a young woman about my age asking the butcher questions. I moved closer and listened. She readily admitted her ignorance and the butcher carefully and patiently told her how to cook a chuck roast.

THE BUTCHER AND ME 13

"That's the answer," I muttered happily to myself. I decided to admit to the butcher that I didn't know much about meat. The man behind the counter came over to me and asked, "Finding what you want, lady?" I hoped he hadn't seen me jump as he spoke.

"Just about. These certainly are nice-looking hams."

"Are you looking for a butt or shank?"

Trapped in my own cleverness, I answered, "It really doesn't matter too much."

"Here's a nice one." He held it up with both hands.

I accepted it even though it was large enough to feed the two of us for a month. "I don't know a lot about cooking. About how much salt should I put on this?" He just shook his head and walked away.

A few years after that three friends and I planned a Christmas party. We shopped together a few days before the party. "Marion," our leader said, "you go get the party ham and have the butcher slice it party thin. Be sure it's not sandwich-sliced."

I didn't attempt to hide my fear. "No, no! Don't make me talk to the butcher. I'll do anything else. Please don't make me talk to *him!*

After they calmed me down, I watched from a safe distance while our leader ordered the ham. I was in my mid-thirties and still couldn't talk to a butcher!

Once I watched a woman ask a butcher to unwrap a package of meat and cut it into certain sizes for her. I thought that was terribly clever. Throwing a pack of pork chops into my cart, I strolled away feeling uncreative.

A few years later while shopping with the twins, who were about three, I discovered a steak sale. Dozens of women stood in line waiting for more steak to be put out. I joined them, feeling very wise. Jon and Jeremy soon became restless in the grocery cart and begged to go home. "What are we waiting for?" one whined. Besides my not knowing how to communicate with the butcher, my twins seemed uncontrollable. It was just too much. I wanted to hold their attention for a while longer so I whispered to them dramatically, "An octopus!" Somehow I thought they'd know I was only teasing.

They sat down and began to wait quietly, wide-eyed with anticipation. Before I could explain I didn't really mean what I said, the child next to us began begging to go home. One of my twins announced at the top of his lungs, "You better wait. My mama says they're gonna bring out an octopus."

I could feel all the women staring at me and the twins. And just then the butcher appeared and glared at me coldly. We strolled on off without the steaks. I tried to smile, but no one smiled back.

Just recently as I shopped I sighed, discovering the chickens weren't cut up the way I'd hoped for. The leg was joined to whatever comes before it. My attempts at cutting up chicken have never worked. Everyone asks at supper, "What happened to the chicken?" I tried not to think about my neighbor who could cut up ten whole chickens in no time flat.

I toyed with the idea of ringing the bell and asking the butcher to cut up the chicken for me. Forty years old, the mother of four, and I still couldn't talk to the butcher. I was older than most of the butchers now. I started to put the chicken back down.

"Pick it up and ring the buzzer," the powerful thought came to my mind. "I'll help you." Of course, the Lord would help me with this ridiculous situation.

I picked the chicken back up, and while I was standing there looking at it, a dear, little old lady who must have been in her eighties walked up and stood by me. She was talking to herself.

I began muttering to myself, somehow hoping she might talk to me. "I wish they'd cut up these chickens," I complained.

"I do too, dear," she smiled at me. "After all they certainly charge enough for them. Why don't you just ring that little buzzer and ask the butcher to do that for you? He does it for me. Go ahead, dear."

I smiled back at her and nearly danced a jig right in the grocery store. *The Lord sent you, dear little lady. Bless you.*

She tottered off still talking to herself, and I rang the bell firmly. It was the first time in almost twenty years of marriage that I'd rung the butcher's bell.

The swinging doors parted and a man who looked like an executioner appeared as if a fire alarm had sounded. I almost threw down the chicken and ran, but remembering I didn't have to do this alone, I said calmly, "Would you please cut this up for me?"

"There's some over there already cut up," he answered gruffly.

Looking him right in the eye, I said, "I looked carefully. I didn't see any."

He marched over and slung chickens around and finally said, "Hey, they are all gone. Sure, I'll cut one for you, lady." He smiled at *me!* I handed him the chicken with triumph. I really hated to cook the chicken; I thought about having it mounted.

The butcher returned and handed me my chicken, now wrapped in brown butcher paper. I put it on the very top of my groceries. When you have meat wrapped in butcher paper, it's obvious you've been talking with the butcher.

It was my own little miracle at the meat counter, and I silently thanked the Lord for giving me victory over my fear of butchers.

# 5

## ON MINISTERING TO A HUSBAND*

In years past I have actually hidden the sports page from my husband or thrown whole newspapers in the trash can. Once I drew a growling frown on the eager, enthusiastic picture of the writer of the sports column that my husband so admires. I've even scribbled notes on the sports page, "Hi there, husband. Why don't you talk to your wife tonight?"

Through the years nothing has worked. Jerry comes in from work, even if it's late after a business meeting, and finds the sports page. Once he got it out of the fireplace and pieced it together at midnight. Another time he went through the garbage can to retrieve it.

Sometimes he reads part of it to me with robust joy, especially if his alma mater is mentioned. He doesn't seem to notice that I'm not listening or never make comments. He reads it to the children and, I suspect, to the dog.

I'm just learning after twenty years of marriage to accept sports as a "normal" part of family life. I resisted bitterly until just recently. Then in desperation I went to the Lord with my dilemma. Miraculously, He's been teaching me as I've been willing to learn. I now know that offense is when we have the ball and defense is when they have the ball. I don't frown at people who scream wildly at games anymore. I'm beginning to understand their enthusiasm, especially since my ten-year-old son gets to run with the ball and usually scores in a game.

But it's been a long, difficult experience for me to accept sports of any kind. I no longer remove the tubes from the TV set when I know an important game is coming on. And I don't jump anymore when my husband bellows and leaps up and down in the den like a

* Originally published as "Jerry 10, Me 1" in *Aglow* magazine. Reprinted by permission.

kangaroo. Sometimes I even look down into the den from the kitchen and smile, "That's nice, dear."

I've learned to insert pads into my sons' uniforms and have accepted going to football and baseball practice every weekday and a game each Saturday as a way of life. Last year I worked on a "footbally" decoration for the little league football banquet.

One pretty day this fall I passed the football with my boys when their daddy was out of town. However, they stopped passing when some of their friends came over to watch.

One of my sons has begun to read the sports page. He looks just like his father hunched over it—smiling slightly.

Maybe if I'd grown up in a home where the father read the sports page, or even if I saw my grandfather do it, the whole thing wouldn't have been so traumatic for me. But my father died before I was two. I had no brothers (or sisters) and no relatives around. When I got married, I really thought that husbands and wives just sat around and talked or read books together. Nothing in life prepared me for the importance that the sports page would have in our marriage.

The other night Jerry came home from work late and really looked tired. It shocked me, because he almost never looks tired. He comes home appearing fresh and smiling, just like he's only been gone about twenty minutes. Sometimes, in reality, it's been twelve hours. He doesn't bring problems about his work home. He never complains (unless he can't find the sports page).

But this one particular night, he looked pale and very tired. He flopped onto the bed and said something about having a terrible headache. Then he mumbled, "Rough day."

I love to minister to people. I suppose one of my spiritual gifts is the one of Helps. But Jerry doesn't often need help. He's pretty self-sufficient and tough. I got a hot cloth and placed it on his head. "Thanks," he said. I kept the hot cloths coming and ran to get two aspirin in between putting cloths on his forehead. Then I sat cross-legged on the bed by him trying to think of something else I could do. I suddenly realized I was grinning and tried to stop. He felt terrible pain and here I sat grinning like a possum. But I so loved being able to do something for him, that I couldn't seem to keep from smiling.

Lord, I prayed, is there something else I can do for my husband? I'll do *anything*.

The Lord spoke to my heart and said, *Yes, you'll be able to further minister to your husband tonight.*

Thrilled, I began to wonder what I could do. Perhaps quote meaningful scripture, pray with him till all hours. Listen to him as he told me about the problems at work. Relate some of my spiritual experiences and victories.

Again, the Lord spoke to me: *You will minister to your husband tonight.*

So, there was something else I was to do. But what? I wanted to talk to him, ask questions, offer suggestions, but something kept me quiet. When Jerry peeped out from under the hot cloth to look at me, I quickly took the smile off my face.

Then, still lying down, he reached over and got the paper off the bedside table. He found the sports page and held it up over him a few inches away from his face. In just a second he dropped it and put the cloth back over his face.

*Minister to your husband,* came the silent suggestion from the Lord.

My smile was really gone then . . . surely . . . surely . . . the Lord wouldn't ask me to do that. Why, that wasn't even . . . spiritual!

*Minister,* came the powerful thought.

"Jerry, would you like for me to read the . . . sports page to you?"

He peeped out at me once more and said, "You wouldn't do that for me. You hate the sports page."

I picked it up and the grinning enthusiastic face that I'd so resented through the years seemed to look right at me. I began reading: "With final results in from the national letter-of-intent deadline, it appears that Tennessee has registered what politicians would call a landslide in football recruiting. Picking up top players in six states, and . . ."

When I finished, Jerry still had the cloth over his eyes, but the expression on the rest of his face had changed. He smiled slightly. Then he said, "Thank you. No one has read me the paper since I was a little boy. That was nice."

He held my hand and patted it a few times, and I started grinning again. I was glad he wasn't looking at me because, of all the silly things, my eyes had filled with tears. I blinked them away, cleared my throat, and read him another column. He finally asked me to stop, but he kept holding my hand. Now I've started putting the paper in an obvious place before Jerry comes home. I listen when he tells me a score. Never mind that I'm not sure if it's football, baseball or basketball. Maybe now that I'm finally learning a little about ministering to my husband, the Lord will show me other unique things I can do for him.

# 6

## HINDS' FEET IN BASEBALL CLEATS*

"Mama," my ten-year-old son, Jon, called from down in the den, "do you think we could pray about the game tonight?"

I was surprised. It was usually I who suggested to my twin sons that we pray about little things—like a ballgame.

I put down the tomato I was slicing and came into the den. "Sure, Jon. I'd love to pray with you." I'd already been praying on my own about the game. Jon played short stop and was good at his position. But tonight he had to pitch. It was only his second time to pitch, and the Yankees were playing a really tough team. Jon's coach was out of town, too.

We'd just discovered that Jon needed new cleats. His toes were pressing against the end of his shoes. My husband had said before he left for work, "Be sure and get Jon new cleats before the game tonight." I nodded. Ordinarily getting a new pair of shoes wouldn't have been a big deal, but we were in between paychecks and had experienced some unexpected medical expenses. I could easily afford the shoes on Friday—payday.

Nevertheless, as soon as Jon and Jeremy came in from school, I said, "Let's go get your cleats, Jon." I explained to Jeremy that he'd get new ones as soon as his wore out. He nodded and decided to stay at home.

Jon and I went in the sports store. He remained unusually quiet. After he tried the shoes on, he asked, "How much are they?" When the clerk told us, he looked quickly at me. I smiled reassuringly. Jon reminded me to ask for the ten-percent discount that was allowed players on local teams. When we got home he laid the shoes out on his bed with his uniform. Then he told me, "They really feel good,

* Originally published as "Jon's Winningest Game" in *Guideposts* magazine, January 1979. Reprinted by permission of *Guideposts* magazine, Copyright 1979 by Guideposts Associates, Inc., Carmel, New York 10512.

Mama, and they're good-looking, too." The only pair of cleats at the store that fit Jon were white. They were nice-looking.

Sitting on the den steps, Jon and I got ready to pray. I suggested, "Why don't we claim some scripture?" Jon understood what I meant. We'd done this before.

"What scripture?" Jon asked.

I guess the scripture about hinds' feet came to my mind because of Jon's new shoes. I answered, "I love the one in Habakkuk 3:19. It's about hinds' feet."

"What kind of feet?" Jon almost laughed.

I explained that hinds were deer that had unusual feet and that they could walk where other animals or even men couldn't walk. I looked for the book *Hinds' Feet on High Places*, but it was loaned out. So I told Jon, "When I have to do something really hard, that could scare me, I remember this scripture and believe that God can give me hinds' feet. That means I can walk in places that would be impossible without God's help. He'll give you hinds' feet too."

He grinned and looked down at his feet. I noticed he needed new Keds, too. I read from the Bible, "The Lord God is my strength, and he will make my feet like hinds' feet, and he will make me to walk upon mine high places."

"The pitcher's mound is a pretty high place," I added, hoping he understood.

"Yeah," Jon smiled. We held hands to pray. Jon held mine so tightly that I almost drew it back. After I prayed, Jon prayed. "God thank you for my new white cleats. Help me do good tonight. Help Tim and Billy and the other boys. And make my feet like . . . hinds' feet tonight."

From the beginning the other team looked great, especially their pitcher. Our fielding was way off. There were several bad calls from the umpires. Jon walked quite a few players. Remembering how much the game meant to him, I kept praying, "Lord, give him hinds' feet."

As I sat watching the game, I realized that I'd never been more proud of Jon. He stood erect, did his best, accepted the bad calls from the umpires. Several times when he pitched to a friend of his on the other team, he smiled, just like he was pitching a no-hit game. I could tell from his enthusiasm that he never gave up hope of winning. When people shouted to him, telling him what he was doing wrong, or openly criticized him, he didn't get angry or frustrated. He kept his mind and his heart on the game. I knew when he dropped his head before a pitch that he was praying.

Jon's team lost sixteen to six.

After it was over he shook hands with the players on the other team and said, "Good game." He didn't complain or blame anyone. He walked away from the field without murmuring. His new shoes were now coated in red dust, and I knew his heart was coated in deep disappointment.

Watching Jon walk toward the car with a slight spring to his step, I thought about the years to come. Other frustrations and agonies inevitably loomed ahead for him. The new cleats would soon be outgrown. But he had countless other shoes to walk in through many difficult situations. One day soon he'd fill the shoes of a teenager, then a husband, a father, someday a businessman. I wondered will he remember the night that God gave him hinds' feet in baseball cleats? Will he remember that God can do it in any situation in life?

I like to think that he will, and someday I hope Jon will tell his son about the night the Yankees lost their ballgame and how he pitched wearing new, white cleats. I hope he'll tell his little boy how God gave him hinds' feet to walk calmly, right through the midst of defeat.

# 7

## THE LONG DISTANCE MIRACLE

Putting the other mail aside, I immediately sat down at my kitchen table to read the letter postmarked West Germany. "You don't know me, but I read your devotional in *Home Life* magazine and decided to write. I want to correspond with an American Christian housewife. Will you write to me?" The rest of the letter told about the writer's happiness in being a new Christian; her husband, two little boys, and life in her homeland, Germany. They had lived in the States at one time. Mostly, it was a cheerful letter. Yet, somehow, in between the lines I sensed a sorrow in this young woman's life. The letter was signed, "Gladys Ross,* Munich, West Germany."

I went to my typewriter and dashed off a two-page letter to Gladys. Her reply came quickly. She wrote: "Please, let's stay in contact. It would mean a lot to me. I don't really know why, but let's do. I still don't know for sure why I wrote to you in the first place. Just felt real strongly that I had to do it . . ." She added: "I believe with all my heart that this is part of our Lord's plan to help me in my present situation. I can't go into detail now but, Marion, I need prayers more than I've ever needed them in my life."

Without knowing specifically what Gladys' need was, I began to pray for her. Sharing bits of our daily lives with each other, we wrote about our children, husbands, busy schedules, and our churches. Gladys seemed especially pleased that we were both Baptist. She wrote that there are almost no Baptists in Germany.

I began to know what to expect toward the end of each of her letters. Some slight reference to an undefined problem. Once she wrote: "I've joined a prayer group, but I can't pray comfortably in German. For me, religion and prayer will always be connected with the States—America. I know that's a mistake, but I can't help it."

Another letter related: "German people are scared stiff to show any feelings—and I am one of them." A few weeks later a letter stated: "In one of your articles, you wrote about friends hugging

* Name changed.

each other. I wish I could do that. I would probably die from embarrassment if someone put their arm around me—even so, it would be nice." Gladys wrote in her next letter that there was a problem in her relationship with her husband.

Then a long lapse. Gladys didn't answer my letters. Over two months passed. Finally a letter arrived. "Marion, certain things can't be put into letters. If only we could talk. Please keep praying for me." She added a P.S.: "Maybe I send you a long distance hug. See, I'm trying to improve."

One Saturday morning I got a letter from Gladys and discovered she now had a part-time job. She wrote: "I'm praying about calling you. Would it be all right if I called you?"

I'd gotten this letter in only four days instead of the usual six, and the mail had come two hours early. I began praying about the possibility of Gladys' calling. I felt God wanted us to talk. Then I wondered if I could understand her German accent and if she could make out my extremely southern one.

My husband took all four of our children on a short shopping trip. How unusual, I marveled. The house is so quiet for a Saturday. I sat on my bed for a moment and wondered what time it was in Germany. Gladys had tried to explain the difference to me, but I'd never understood it. She could be asleep now. I began praying for her anyway.

The phone interrupted.

"Hello," I answered.

Very clearly I heard: "Hello, Mrs. West, this is Gladys Ross calling."

"Gladys!" I screamed and jumped up to a standing position. I couldn't believe we were actually talking. I'd never talked to anyone in another country before. There was no static, and we didn't have to raise our voices. Our connection was so beautiful that it was as if she was only across the street. We began by making small talk. She started calling me Marion, instead of Mrs. West. Gladys was calling from her office. She was alone there and could talk. It was 6:45 P.M. in Germany and 12:45 P.M. in Georgia. Gladys said it was raining in Germany. "It is here too," I said excitedly, glancing out the window.

Then Gladys' tone of voice changed, "I'm at my rope's end, Marion. Something is very wrong with my marriage, my relationship to Jesus. Something is wrong with me. I'm so unhappy. I've never been so desperate or frightened."

I voiced some kind, appropriate words, but way in the back of my mind, I thought, *Lord, what can I do? We're an ocean apart and strangers. And, things aren't too great in my own life today. I've felt separated from You this week. Why, of all people in the world, is she calling me? My faith isn't big enough to share today. There's not even enough for me.*

I wanted to help Gladys so much that tears brimmed my eyes. The situation seemed impossible. She was waiting for me to say something. I felt a gentle nudging from God and knew what He wanted me to do. I didn't feel like doing it. Nevertheless, I heard myself say, "Gladys, could I pray with you?"

"Oh, yes, please do."

Without any emotion or feeling, I asked the Holy Spirit to fill Gladys. I asked Jesus to heal her marriage. I asked Him to help her love her husband, children, and people in her church in a wonderful new way. I prayed that Gladys might even love strangers. And then I asked Jesus to help Gladys love herself. I could have been saying the ABC's as far as my emotions were concerned.

"Thank you," she said simply.

I looked out the window and watched the rain beating against the pane. Everything looked gray and hopeless. My already tiny faith seemed to shrink away rapidly like the light on a television screen when it's turned off. *How foolish of me to think I could pray across an ocean with a stranger.*

We talked on and suddenly Gladys interrupted and asked in a hushed voice: "Marion, are you positive that Jesus can heal a marriage? Give me a new love for my husband—for people—even for myself?"

"Yes," I responded quickly, halfway expecting her to disagree with me. "I'm certain He can do that."

"Then I'm going to do something now. Only you and I and Jesus know about it. This moment I surrender everything to Jesus. My life, my will, my bitterness, my marriage, my inability—to love. I'm broken in two. I give myself, all of me, to Jesus. Total surrender. Selling out—you know?"

Such powerful feelings of joy and deep emotion erupted in my pounding heart that I thought I couldn't possibly utter a word. Choking back tears, I said, "Yes, yes! I know!"

She was laughing, maybe crying too. Her voice sounded different. "Something has been lifted from me. My troubles are gone. Oh, Marion, I'm so happy—really for the first time. Jesus is working a miracle in me right now. He's even giving me the ability to speak to you in good English. I can't speak English so good." Finally Gladys said: "I've got to go now. I want to leave work early. I have to see my husband. I believe Jesus has another miracle for me today."

"Gladys, I love you for calling," I said quickly before she hung up.

A moment's hesitation. Then she answered, "I think—yes, I believe I do love you too. Write me today."

The line went dead. I stared out the window, crying uncontrollably. The rain didn't appear gray anymore. Trees, grass, housetops, even the telephone lines seemed to glisten. I felt new, vibrant faith in my own heart.

In Gladys' next letter, she wrote: "I really did totally surrender to Jesus. I went home to my husband and gave him a hug and a kiss! Jesus went with me.

"You remember you told me it's important to tell people you love them. You said to hug someone. Well, Jesus made it clear that I was to hug two women in my church and tell them I loved them. I looked for them (hoping not to see them) but I went up to one and she hugged me *first!* I hugged her back. We tell each other, 'I love you.' Then we both cry. But it was okay.

"The other person was the preacher's wife. I walked right up to her and said, 'I appreciate you, and I love you.' Marion, this was an experience like I never have before. I also prayed publicly for the first time. You remember, you told me to go forward and surrender publicly? Well, Germans don't do this. It's not our custom. The thought of going up front during the invitation scared me stiff. But *I went.*

"Guess there aren't many long distance miracles like I had. Love and a big hug, Gladys."

Gladys' long distance miracle constantly reminds me of a tremendous truth: God's power isn't limited by my feelings.

# 8

## MY MARVELOUS FIFTEEN-CENT DISCOVERY

That sinking feeling that I was going to have to do the impossible began when my eighteen-year-old daughter, Julie, told her daddy and me, "I have to go downtown to the *Journal* office."

She'd been selected the senior recipient of the *Journal* Cup, and winners from all the high schools were asked to come to the newspaper office in downtown Atlanta to have pictures taken.

My husband's schedule and Julie's were such that it was impossible for him to take her. She didn't know how to drive downtown by herself. In the six years that we'd lived in the Atlanta area, I'd never driven into the city. I have absolutely no sense of direction, and a childlike fear of getting lost lurks deep within me.

Julie and Jerry both looked at me. When Julie saw my face she said, "Let's just forget about the picture." I smiled a little.

My husband said, "No, Julie, you should go, and it's time your mother figured how to go downtown. Other mothers do it." Then in a softer tone he explained that I could drive to a familiar point, the Gulf station, and simply take the Marta Bus from there. "It's simple. Anyone can get on a bus."

On the morning of our big bus trip, I awoke early, with something fluttering around in my stomach like butterflies. Julie and I left before eight. I confessed to her as we drove, "Your daddy tried to give me taxi money—just in case . . ."

"Mother! He said you could do this."

"I can. I can. I can," I mumbled to myself.

At the bus stop, clutching our two fifteen-cent fares, I realized that I didn't know which bus to take. Jerry hadn't told me. "Ask that man," Julie encouraged. I didn't want to appear ignorant, but finally, I asked casually, I hoped, "You going downtown?"

He nodded. Looked like he caught the bus every morning. Very cool in his pin-striped suit and dark glasses. I decided to forget about the name of the bus. I'd just get on the same bus he got on. I asked instead, "Does it go by the *Journal* office?"

"Goes within four blocks."

"You mean I have to find the office?"

He stared at me intently for a moment, then said, slowly, "Do you know where the little park is, near Five Points?"

I made the decision to be completely honest, even if it meant letting Julie see me at my worst. "I don't know where anything is!"

He started giving directions, and I didn't attempt to understand them. Getting on the right bus would be good enough for now. "Anyway," I reasoned, "Julie has a good sense of direction. She wouldn't be getting the *Journal* Cup if she wasn't smart. She'll know what to do."

Julie leaned over and touched my arm, "Mother, I'm glad you know where we're going. This is scary."

A bus approached. Suddenly I remembered that Jerry had told me the name of the bus to catch—Medlock. And here it came. I was so excited that I nearly jumped up and down and hollered, "Here it comes, everybody." But the other riders appeared so casual, that I just quietly got in the line, hoping I looked as cool as the man in the dark glasses.

I asked the driver, cautiously, before sitting down, "Do you go near the *Journal* office?"

"Within four blocks. Do you know where the little park . . ."

"I don't know where anything is," I admitted once again.

He looked at me for a moment, then he seemed to mentally put me into a category. I didn't care. He smiled at me and said reassuringly, "I'll tell you when to get off." Julie and I sat right behind the driver (so he wouldn't forget us) and I noticed we were in the handicapped section.

Julie had marveled that I knew how much money to put in the collection box, and that had given me a little confidence.

We suddenly both stared in amazement at a little boy about ten riding the bus alone to school. He looked sleepy and relaxed. His feet didn't even touch the floor. "Mother, sit back and relax. Look casual," Julie whispered. "You look nervous." I quickly slumped and tried to look bored.

The little boy pulled the bell and got off at his stop. Julie and I both stared out the window at him till he was out of sight.

"All these people do this every day," she whispered to me, as we looked around at all the people. I nodded, admiring each one.

Finally, we were downtown and I became certain the driver had forgotten about us. "Ask him," Julie nudged me. Smiling and trying to be flip, I said loudly, "'Bout our stop?"

"Coming up," he replied and I felt great. The man in the dark glasses looked at us like he was impressed.

As we started off the bus, the driver instructed, "Walk straight ahead for three traffic lights. When you see a big statue in the middle of the street, it's the next building on the left."

Realizing that I was holding up the line of people trying to exit, I asked, "How do we get back to where we came from?"

"Catch the Medlock Number 12."

"Thanks," I answered too loudly.

We got off the bus and blended into the throng of rapidly moving people. We walked grimly and swiftly until we saw the statue, then we both squealed for joy. Entering the enormous *Journal* building, we relaxed as though we were going to McDonald's.

People at the *Journal* directed us cheerfully and promptly to the proper place. Within a few minutes, we left the building, our mission accomplished. As we walked onto the street once again, we both said at the exact time, "Now take a right."

Safely back at the spot where we'd gotten off the bus, we relaxed until we realized that we should be standing somewhere else in order to go in the opposite direction. Mainly I remembered because once I'd stood on the wrong side of the street for an hour and a half for a bus.

When the next bus came by, I darted inside and blurted out, "How do I catch the Medlock Number 12?"

The driver began telling me, but such a confused look must have crossed my face that he smiled and seemed to mentally place me in "that" category again. "Just stand still, lady, where you are. I'll take you to it." I called out the door for Julie. She hurried aboard, and I continued to stand as close to the driver as I could get. "Mother, you look like a first grader. Sit down," she urged. I sat on the edge of a seat, ready to exit at a moment's notice. In a few seconds the driver opened the door and smiled again, "Wait right here."

When we got off, the first thing we saw was a big orange-and-blue sign with buses listed on it. Medlock Number 12 was the third bus on the big sign. There were no benches, so we sat on a concrete step with some boys and watched people getting on and off buses. I told Julie, "Some people ask for transfers and change buses—go all the way across the city."

"You're kidding," she said.

Just then a man about eighty came up and asked if we could help him get on the Stone Mountain bus. It was listed with the other buses. He said he couldn't see to read. We were delighted to be able to help someone and get him on his bus.

Feeling more secure now, we boarded the Medlock Number 12, sitting right behind the driver again in the handicapped section. After a while Julie said, "I remember this railroad track," as we bumped across it.

"And I remember that yellow house." Convinced that we were on the right bus, we settled back and made small talk like regular commuters.

Just then the young driver turned and with a half grin on his face said to us, "I just made a wrong turn."

I wanted to say something that wouldn't reveal that I didn't know the way home either, so I said, "I didn't think you drivers ever did that."

"It's my first day," he beamed enthusiastically.

"Ours too," Julie said under her breath and grabbed for my hand.

Finally, our stop loomed ahead. We stepped off the bus and I sighed, "I feel like we've been to the moon."

Julie nodded. "I can't believe people do this every day."

Back in our green station wagon, we drove to a little restaurant two miles from our house. The expressway, the Waffle House, the menu, even the waitress all looked sweetly familiar. Eating breakfast, I said, "Know something, Julie?"

"What?"

"I never knew till today that the smartest thing you can do when you don't know how to do something is just to admit it. Almost forty-two years old, and I just learned that. You know, it wasn't just the two of us that rode that bus. The Lord went with us. Imagine! He'll even ride a bus with you. That's a marvelous fifteen-cent discovery, don't you think?"

She nodded. "Pretty good advice for a graduating senior, too. I'll remember it . . . and today. Thanks, Mom."

# 9

## BUT I CAN'T SPEAK, LORD

I knew instinctively what the smiling woman was about to ask me to do. Maybe I'm wrong, I hoped. *Oh, please, Lord, don't let her ask me to speak to this group.*

"Marion, we're so thrilled about your book. Won't you come and speak to our book review club? As you can see, it's just a small, informal group of friends. You can even sit down."

I was back at my home church for a visit. About eighteen women, many of them elderly, sat in a circle in the church library. They smiled a lot. I'd known most of them all my life. They loved me. I loved them. And I loved my hometown, my home church. Right that moment I loved everything and everyone—except the idea of speaking to anyone about anything. Several of the older women encouraged me. One put her arm around me. "You can do it. Anybody who can write a book can speak. Will you come?"

They all looked at me and waited for my answer. All of me desperately wanted to say a flat no. Speaking terrified me to a point of being ridiculous. I didn't even like to say my name when a roomful of people introduced themselves.

I'd recently told the Lord that I'd do anything He asked. But deep in my heart, there were two reservations. Flying was one—and already since I'd promised to be obedient to Him, I'd had to fly. The other was speaking. Surely, He wouldn't ask me to do that too!

I heard myself say, "Yes, ma'am. I'll come, but I'm not a speaker like the lady you had here today." I tried to laugh, but my mouth was too dry. "Yes, the second Tuesday in February will be fine."

She smiled. "You'll do fine. Just fine."

Back at home in my kitchen, I wrote on my calendar: "Speak to book review club in Elberton." Then I stood back and read what I'd written. Seeing it in writing frightened me even more. But then, it was just November. Maybe by February the fear would go away. Never mind that I'd had it all my life. Maybe it would be gone by February. Maybe God would just take it away since I was being so obedient.

About January I began to think (or maybe pray) that we might just have an ice storm on the second Tuesday in February. "This is a rough winter. I couldn't drive to Elberton in bad weather. They wouldn't expect me to. Someone else could speak. Maybe if I'm just *willing* to go, the Lord won't really make me go. Being willing is important.

The second Tuesday in February dawned clear and sunny. I didn't even need a coat. At 3 A.M. I had awakened gripped in terror. I hadn't known fear like this since I'd given the Lord complete charge of my life four years earlier. The overpowering thought that Christians aren't supposed to be afraid came crashing into my mind and I felt guilty on top of being afraid. "I can't do it, Lord. I can't," I whispered in the darkness.

In the midst of my fear, I remembered what I'd been taught at a conference we were having at our church. The speaker had emphasized that we must praise God, *no matter what*. Especially if things are going bad, we should praise Him. It had sounded good in the daylight with everyone sitting around smiling and unafraid. It sounded goofy, however, in the middle of the night when fear had plopped right down on my chest.

The speaker had emphasized that if we don't know how to pray, we can simply, in childlike faith, praise the Lord. I didn't know how to pray anymore, and I didn't know a lot about praising the Lord. But the fear seemed to be smothering me. Careful not to awaken my husband, I began humming, "Let's just praise the Lord." I thought about the words as I hummed. Then I hummed, "Alleluia." I was still afraid. I began to think and hum, "I will praise Him. I will thank Him. I will love Him." Finally, "I will trust Him."

For nearly two hours I praised the Lord by humming softly in bed or simply thinking about those songs. The fear didn't disappear.

Later that morning it greeted me before I opened my eyes. I got out of bed singing, "Let's just praise the Lord." The speaker had said not to quit if we felt like it, and I sure felt like it.

I got our four children off to school, my husband off to work, and fed our four cats as I continued to sing softly the songs of praise.

Driving over to pick up a friend, Venera, who had planned to go with me, I sang, "Alleluia." By now I was singing it loudly. It didn't matter that I was tone deaf. I stopped singing, however, when Venera got in the car, because she sings well and on key. I just kept thinking the songs to myself. Just as we approached Elberton, Venera began singing softly, "Let's just praise the Lord." I grinned a little and joined in, off-key, still frightened, but nevertheless praising Him.

I was greeted warmly at the church and we headed toward the library. But to my surprise we walked right past it. I peeked in. No one was there. "Oh, Father," I thought wildly, "no one has come. I was willing, but I don't have to do it. How wonderful Your ways are." I waited for the woman to explain to me that no one had come.

She started talking enthusiastically, "We're meeting in another room, Marion. We put a little article in the paper about your coming to speak and it drew quite a crowd." She opened double doors, and I walked into an enormous room packed full of people. It looked like thousands to me.

Suddenly I remembered the story in the Bible about the little boy who had a small lunch of fish and bread. I identified with him now. My little speech couldn't possibly feed all these people.

*Oh, Lord, what am I going to do?* People came up to speak to me. There were old friends, teachers from high school, relatives and strangers. My mouth was so dry I couldn't swallow and my heart pounded. Venera kept smiling at me. An old friend came up and said, "Marion, I didn't know you could speak. I'd never do it in front of all these people. I admire your courage."

I smiled weakly and bellowed out another silent prayer, *I don't have any courage, Lord. Help me! I'm helpless.*

He seemed to say to me, *Forget about your speech that you've worked so hard on. Forget the little prayer you've written out. Make your mind blank and I'll fill it.*

Someone began to introduce me. Someone else prayed. It was my time to go to the speaker's stand. I walked over with my Bible and

an outline of a speech. I smiled and thought, what in the world do I
have to smile about. Then mentally I tore up my notes and said, *All
right, Lord, my mind's blank. Give me something to say.*

New thoughts eased into my mind rapidly and faithfully as if
they came from a ticker tape. Some of the thoughts I didn't want to
share, but I didn't hesitate a second. The thoughts might stop coming if I didn't speak them quickly. I said things I had no intention
of saying—even felt foolish saying. I was faintly aware that I was
standing and speaking, and yet it seemed as if I were over in a safe
corner watching, listening. I smiled a lot and used my hands.

Some of it must have been funny, because people laughed, and
they wouldn't have laughed if it wasn't okay—not in my own hometown.

All those people seemed to blend into one person who listened
and understood and nodded and encouraged. Way in the back of
my mind a tiny thought came, a thought that I wasn't to say out
loud. I just marveled over it. I was having fun!

An hour passed. How quickly it has gone by. They had said I
was to speak for an hour. It was almost over. The idea came to me
to allow time for questions. I didn't feel like I knew the answer to
anything, but I asked if there were any questions. I didn't even
know what I had said. I hoped no one would ask something I didn't
remember talking about.

Of all that was said and asked that day, this one question stands
out in my mind. It was the first question asked.

"You speak and write about new kinds of freedom through Jesus.
What is the one freedom that means the most to you?"

I knew the answer before she finished the question and I started
smiling and praising the Lord in my heart. I answered quickly,
"The freedom to fail."

I finally sat down in awe. I had made a speech! I wondered what
I'd said. While people came by to speak to me and say nice things,
I praised the Lord silently in my heart. I felt like praising Him
now. He knew all along I couldn't speak and would have to depend
upon Him.

# IO

## I'VE GOT THE BLAHS AGAIN

I'd rather have the flu or an ingrown toenail than the blahs. Not that I really want to have anything. But if I must suffer, I'd rather have something that can be diagnosed and treated.

With the flu I know what I can and can't do. Activities are limited to bed rest, reading, and talking on the phone. My prayer is specific. *Lord, my nose is stopped up and my head hurts just behind my left eye. Please stop it.*

With an ingrown toenail I know I can walk if absolutely necessary with my toe turned up. And certainly I'm aware of where it hurts, and pray, *Lord, my left big toe hurts.* I know where healing is needed.

But with the blahs, I don't know where I hurt. There's sort of a sadness in my heart that moves around. A stop-and-go headache attacks. My limbs hang unenthusiastically. Temper is short and nasty. Everything appears futile. Joy seems to have flown from my soul.

Rainy weather or a cloudy day is a good prerequisite for the blahs. Or too much leisure time. But then so is too much that must be done. There's just no pattern to it. Whining children, spilled Kool-Aid, a shower of crumbs under the kitchen table, a glance in the mirror at my fallen hair, spider webs on the ceiling, and a pile of ironing add to the blahs—but do not cause them. I have never, once, known the cause or cure.

The blahs seem to be a sneaky illness, striking without warning. Sometimes I try to read my way out of the blahs but can't. Don't want to concentrate. Think of phoning a friend, but don't want to talk or even dial the phone. Cleaning out closets is out of the question; so is walking across the room.

Exuberant children running and tumbling in the back door and out the front door, while firing questions at me, worsen my deteriorating condition. "Go outdoors," I plead for the umpteenth time, feeling even worse now—knowing somewhere there are mothers who bend down smiling, brush their child's hair back and murmur, "Of course, I'll come out and look at the fuzzy caterpillar. Then we'll look him up in the World Book. How's that, little buckaroo?"

Usually when the blahs attack I sit on the sofa like Raggedy Ann, staring at the places under the TV I missed when I waxed. Upon arising, I walk around the house looking out windows, listening to children opening and shutting doors, including the refrigerator.

Thoughts of preparing supper are unthinkable. I almost wish I could go to bed with a diagnosed case of the flu, or rest on the sofa nursing an inflamed toenail.

I force myself to plug in the iron, then jerk the cord out of its connection. I don't have any energy. Gazing hopefully out the window, I search for the appearance of the sun. The day is gray. I glance at the clock wondering if it's been unplugged too.

I never seem to have the blahs on days when I know I must drive three car pools, or meet a friend for lunch, or on Thursdays (I go to the beauty shop on Thursday) or I'm expecting company. I've gotten a sudden case of the blahs when my husband was out of town and I let the house, myself, and the children "go" all day.

My husband knows as soon as he comes home from work and our eyes meet if I have the blahs, and he looks away and pretends he doesn't notice. I see him thinking, *Uh oh, she's got "it" again. One of those moods.* His attempts to avoid me only make the blahs worse.

Doing the supper dishes alone tonight, a revelation dawned on me. And I smiled for the first time all day. Maybe God allows the blahs to draw me to Him. I find myself talking to Him more when I have a good case of the blahs than on those days when I am relying fully on MYSELF and MY abilities.

*I just can't cope with the blahs, Lord. Everyone avoids me. I don't blame 'em. I don't like to be around me either. I wish I could turn away from myself. But You, Lord, You hang in there with me—just as though I'm fun to be with. You're the only one who does.*

*Thanks.*

## II

# WHAT'S LAY RENEWAL, ANYWAY?

I'd heard the term Lay Renewal floating around. Some Christians I knew spoke about it with great enthusiasm. I'd read glowing accounts of lives being changed at a Lay Renewal experience. But I didn't know exactly what happened. I was more than mildly interested in attending a Lay Renewal. When our pastor mentioned one to Jerry and me, I knew immediately I wanted to go but smiled and decided to leave the decision up to Jerry.

Jerry told me later that he didn't think he could get away from the office that weekend, and I thought, "You don't know what Lay Renewal is either, and you're not sure you even want to go." But I smiled before the disappointment registered on my face and prayed, "Okay, Lord. Please change my wanter. I wanna go and I don't think he does."

Right away I decided it would be a lot of trouble leaving the children, and anyway I wasn't so sure what Lay Renewal was either. So, smiling, I answered, "Okay." I told the pastor I didn't think we could go but that Jerry hadn't said definitely. Then just before the deadline for getting in reservations, Jerry announced in the middle of supper that we were going. My desire to go returned immediately, and with great enthusiasm I turned in our names.

Jerry and I were happy about attending. Actually I was almost hysterical that we were going somewhere—*anywhere*—without the children. But before we reached the outskirts of town, we weren't speaking and I'd sulked way over to my side of the car feeling the tremendous wall that had sprung up between us. Jerry drove intently, hunched over the wheel, not even glancing my way.

The argument was as old as our marriage of seventeen years. He'd been late getting home from the office and we were an hour behind schedule. For him five o'clock could mean anywhere from five fifteen to five forty-five. To me it meant no later than ten minutes before five.

We arrived in Toccoa, Georgia, speaking politely whenever necessary or smiling when a stranger spoke to us. Most everybody was already there, and I was sure we'd missed something. I searched the large room for someone I thought I'd like to get to know. As I looked about, no one seemed to leap out at me or even look interesting and I felt a stab of disappointment. The whole weekend was going to be a disaster. I wished we hadn't come.

Lay Renewals must be one of Satan's favorite stomping grounds!

In our room I unpacked furiously to compensate for the silence between us. I took my Bible and went into the bathroom fighting back tears and prayed, asking God to give me something to calm me down. And I read in Psalms 130:6, "My soul waiteth for the Lord" (KJV).

I felt a little better, but I hated to wait on anything or anyone. Waiting seemed to be one of the most difficult areas of my life. So naturally the Lord was going to teach me something about waiting. I'd wanted to learn about something else—anything else.

I didn't learn easily. At supper I still searched for someone I thought would be fun to share with. Everyone looked quite ordinary—some people, even dull. Many didn't look like Christians, I decided.

Just about that time a friendly man introduced himself to us. As he and Jerry talked, my eyes went to the Jesus sticker he wore on his shirt. I decided right away that I didn't want to get into a sharing group with him. He was too pushy. I loved Jesus too, but I didn't wear a Jesus sticker. Jerry didn't seem to notice the sticker. I smiled politely and pretended to be interested in what he said.

We gathered in the chapel after supper. I liked it. Small, warm, friendly, with a tiny altar, gleaming pews, and sliding glass doors. Walking to the chapel at dusk we heard the crickets and frogs begin their night song, and the scent of pine trees was strong. God seemed close. I didn't have any children to get to bed. Maybe the weekend wouldn't be a flop after all.

About ninety of us sat in the chapel, and to my horror I looked up and saw that the man I didn't want to get to know was the leader of the Lay Renewal weekend, Fred Roach!

In the first three minutes he spoke, my attitude changed. He spoke informally, gently—yet powerfully. He encouraged us to have fun, to call one another by first names, and to love each other.

Love was to be the theme for the weekend. I looked at Jerry out of the corner of my eye. Fred continued speaking. He didn't use humdrum language or flaunt his knowledge of the Scripture. He possessed a marvelous sense of humor, humility, and enthusiasm. In just a few moments I'd come to admire and love this man with the Jesus sticker.

Fred said, "God wants such an intense relationship with us that we should be so tuned in to Him that we know what He wants just as we feel what our mate wants when they give us a certain look." I looked over at Jerry just in time to catch him looking at me. We got tickled and had to use a lot of effort not to start laughing. Our argument and anger had vanished, like a popped balloon.

We broke into sharing groups. The leader spoke briefly, and we introduced ourselves and somehow became instant friends. There was no pressure put on anyone (except by the Holy Spirit) to share. Everyone in the group did share, however. Some of the prayer requests were:

1. "Pray for my husband. He has a wonderful testimony but gets so emotional he can't speak. And my son is at a crossroads in his life."

2. "Pray for my husband and me. We have two children, and the Lord has called him into the ministry. I'm too shy and uneducated to be a minister's wife. I don't know how we'll make it financially."

3. "I'm one year old in the Lord. I have a third-grade education, and I'm teaching tenth-grade boys in Sunday school. I want to work in Bible school and am an alcoholic. Pray for me."

4. "I'm not yet twenty. I need to know God's will for my vocation. I have to make an important decision next week."

5. "Pray that I can leave my husband alone and let God work with him."

On and on they went. As each request was shared, we stopped and prayed before going on. While someone spoke, others smiled, nodded—understood and cared.

Back in the chapel we all met together again. Everyone looked different. They had a—glow. I felt different. None of the people appeared ordinary anymore. A speaker from each group shared. Some of the comments were:

1. "We have decided to follow Jesus."
2. "Actions speak louder than words."
3. "Let the Holy Spirit take control of your life."
4. "Show others you love them—don't be afraid to love others."
5. "We should bear one another's burdens."
6. "Let's be joyful Christians."
7. "This was the most spiritual thing I've ever been involved in."
8. "The Lord put our group together."
9. "Amazing how we shared knowing each other only a few minutes. The Holy Spirit was our leader."
10. "Be yourself."
11. "Walk in the Spirit."

Right then we were asked to turn and tell someone near us that God loved them and we did too. I turned around, smiled at Fred Roach (Jesus sticker and all), and said, "I love you. God does too."

Then we divided into another sharing group and Satan insisted, "You won't get another group like that first one." I was a bit surprised to see that I and another woman were in a group of men. Sharing with men was new for me, and I felt myself becoming apprehensive.

"Oh, me," I thought, "these men won't say anything. This other woman and I will have to do all the talking for an hour." Actually, we two women had to be quick to get a word in! I realized then that men and women aren't so different. Men hurt, are afraid, rejoice too.

A minister in the group asked us to pray for total surrender for him. "I'm still holding back. I know I am," he almost whispered. "I can't surrender completely. I want to."

Our leader suggested that we split up into twos and go outside and pray with our partner. I felt sure that the other woman and I would be partners. But I got our leader for a partner. How would I pray with a man—a complete stranger? We sat down together on a picnic bench while a curious squirrel watched us. We prayed with our eyes open after we shared some of the needs in our lives. His eyes brimmed slightly with tears, and I felt somehow comfortable with him.

Back in the chapel people were sharing. The minister who'd been in our group stood and announced quite simply that he'd said to God, "Here I am, Lord. All of me. Use me." He added that he'd felt no tremendous feelings—no lightning flashed, but he'd meant it—finally. Now he knew he was totally surrendered.

Someone shared: "Fathers, love your wives. It's the greatest thing you can do for your children."

Another: "Don't criticize your church till your home is in better shape."

Another: "It's not your works—it's your surrender that counts."

My favorite remains: "I tried for years to rededicate a life that had never been dedicated. Finally, I just gave all of me to God. Then there was no need to rededicate."

Miracles come in all sizes. I shared that for the first time in seventeen years Jerry was ready that morning before I was and he waited for me! The group laughed and applauded. Someone reached over and touched me as they rejoiced with me.

Together for the last time as a group we joined hands and sang, "God Is So Good," "Fill Me, Jesus," and "In Our Home, Lord, We Praise Thee."

Lay Renewal was over. We said good-bye to dear friends. Some people stood around sharing or praying together. A young man who'd been in one of my groups came running up to me. He was a minister. Tears filled his eyes. "She did it," he told me. "My wife finally totally surrendered. She's been so afraid of it for so long. She's so happy she can't stop smiling, and she's not afraid to be a minister's wife anymore. Keep praying for her and me."

I nodded joyfully. Jerry and I drove off waving a last good-bye to new friends. We were silent most of the way home, but we were close together in thoughts. We held hands for miles.

Back at home as we drove into the driveway, I wondered, am I really different? Just then I spotted a neighbor—an unbeliever—who'd poked fun at us for going to church so often. I usually avoided him because I didn't like his teasing, gruff manner. But without a second thought, I ran over, touched him on the shoulder and said, "Hey."

He looked up, jumped slightly, cut off the lawn mower and said, "Hello."

"Jesus loves you and I do too," I shouted, not realizing he'd cut off the lawn mower. His mouth fell open and he shouted back, "What's happened to you?"

"I've been to Lay Renewal." I lowered my voice. I almost added, "and I'm not afraid of you anymore."

He grinned. "Well get away from me. My wife went to one of those, and now she acts funny." But he said it in a warm, friendly way, and his smiling eyes didn't agree with what his mouth insisted.

I sighed. I wasn't a bit afraid of him anymore. The wall between us had come tumbling down. "Bye," I said and ran back across the street.

He waved. Running into my front yard, I remembered all the times I'd started over to his house to witness to him if it killed me. All those times I'd never liked him, and I'm sure he knew it.

AUTHOR'S NOTE: Four years after the Lay Renewal, Jerry and I were on a couples' retreat five hundred miles from our home. There we met the young minister and his wife once again. He looked just the same, but I hardly recognized his wife. Her joy and peace radiated across the room. She confirmed when I asked her, "Yes, that Lay Renewal was the beginning of a new kind of life for me. It was the beginning of death to myself. Oh, it was terribly painful to die, but well worth the cost. I've been set free from fear. At last I know who I am." She added, "My miracles have been quiet, gentle—but miracles nevertheless." She was one of the most completely transformed people I've ever seen.

# 12

## DOES GOD CARE ABOUT LOST DOGS?

The bitter, cold weather had forced the large, red dog to curl into a tighter ball, tucking his nose under his big, muddy feet. Old Red lived outside Larry's Barber Shop, sleeping on a small scrap of carpeting. The mongrel dog had panted through a hot summer, watching hopefully as the children came out of the small grocery store that adjoined the barber shop. Many shared their treats with him.

On Valentine's Day I saw a handful of candy hearts that had been left on the carpet for Old Red.

Old Red once had a buddy—a scrawny black dog. Constant companions, they slept curled together. During a cold spell the smaller dog disappeared. Old Red mourned his friend by keeping his usually wagging tail motionless. As friends stooped to pat him, Old Red wouldn't even look up.

Someone dumped a puppy out one day, and Old Red immediately adopted him. He followed the puppy around like a mother hen. During the cold nights Old Red shared his carpet with the frisky puppy, letting him sleep against the wall. Old Red slept on the cold outside.

Soon that puppy disappeared too, and the old dog was alone again.

I would have taken him home in a minute. Any homeless dog or cat could win my instant friendship. All it took was one hopeful look.

But my husband had explained time and time again that we simply could not take in stray animals. I knew he was right. But sometimes my heart forgot.

With great determination I tried to steel myself against looking into the eyes of any stray, hungry dog or cat. Old Red never looked hungry, though, so I decided it was all right to form a relationship with him.

One day I found out by accident from the barber's wife that her husband was feeding the dog daily. "He won't even buy cheap food," she laughed, "buys the most expensive there is."

I stopped by the barber shop to tell Larry how grateful I was that he was feeding the dog. He brushed aside my thanks and insisted the dog meant nothing to him. "I'm thinking of having him taken off," Larry mumbled gruffly.

He didn't fool me a bit.

During a snowstorm Old Red disappeared. I haunted the barber shop. "Larry, where can he be?" I'd ask.

"I'm glad he's gone. He was a bother, and it was getting expensive feeding him," Larry insisted as he continued cutting a customer's hair without looking at me.

Later Larry's wife told me he had driven for miles looking for the dog. On the third day the dog reappeared. I ran to him and patted his head. The big, dirty tail didn't flop once. He didn't even raise his head. I felt his nose. Hot and dry! Bursting into the barber shop, I hollered, "Larry, Old Red's sick!"

Larry continued cutting a customer's hair. "I know. Won't eat."

"Where do you think he's been?"

"I can't prove it, but I think someone at the shopping center complained and he was hauled off. Did you see his feet? Looks like he's been walking for days to get back."

I lowered my voice, "Let him inside, Larry."

The customers seemed to be enjoying our conversation.

"I can't do that. This is a place of business."

I left the shop, and for hours I tried to get someone involved in helping Old Red. The Humane Society said they'd take the dog. But they were an hour's drive across Atlanta, and I had no idea how to get there. Anyway, no one would adopt a sick dog, and they'd put him to sleep. A vet I phoned said right away that he didn't take charity cases. The police, fire department, and manager of the shopping center could offer no help. None of my friends was interested.

I knew I was about to bring Old Red home despite my husband's rules about strays. I hadn't brought an animal home in a long time.

As I fixed supper that night I said very little. My husband finally asked grimly, "Do you want me to go look at that dog with you?" Translated this meant, "I'll get involved a little bit. But we cannot have the dog."

"Oh yes." I ran to the attic and got a large box and a blanket. Grabbing some aspirin and an antibiotic one of the children had been taking, and warming some milk, I finally announced, "I'm ready."

Snow covered the ground. We piled our four children in the car and started for the shopping center. *Hold on, Old Red. We're coming.*

As we entered the shopping center all my hopes faded. He was gone. "Oh, he's gone off to die," I moaned. We drove around and looked and called, but the dog didn't come.

The next day I took the boys in for a haircut. Old Red was back! But he looked worse than ever. After feeling his hot nose, I ran quickly into the barber shop. "Larry, the dog is going to die right in front of your shop."

Larry liked to tease me—even about this. He didn't look up. "Think he's already dead. Haven't seen him move all morning."

"Larry," I screamed, "you've got to do something!"

I left the barber shop with a heavy heart. It took all my will power not to put Old Red in our car. He seemed resigned to his fate. I was almost in tears. One of my twins kept asking me something as we sat in our car. He repeated his question for the third time.

"Does God care about lost dogs, Mama?"

I knew I had to answer Jeremy even though God seemed far away. I felt a little guilty, too, because I never thought about bothering God with this. "Yes, Jeremy, God cares about all His creatures." I was afraid of his next question.

"Then let's ask Him to make Old Red well. Can we do that, Mama?"

"Of course, Jeremy," I answered somewhat exasperated. What else could I say to a five-year-old?

Jeremy bowed his head, folded his hands, shut his eyes, and said, "God, I want to ask You to make Old Red well again. And please . . . send a little boy to love him. Amen."

Jeremy waited patiently for my prayer. I felt like explaining to him that animals were suffering everywhere. But I prayed, "Dear Lord, thank You for caring about all Your creatures. Please send someone to care about Old Red. Please hurry."

Jon added his prayer to ours, and I backed out of the parking place. I was crying now, but Jeremy and Jon didn't seem to notice. Jeremy let down the window and called out cheerfully, "Bye, Old Red. You're gonna be okay. Someone's coming to get you."

The tired old dog raised his head slightly as we drove off.

Two days later Larry called. "Guess what," he said.

I was afraid to ask.

"Your dog's well."

"What . . . how . . ."

There was unmistakable excitement in Larry's voice. "Yesterday a vet came in to have his hair cut, and I asked him to take a look at the dog—cause you were about to drive me crazy. Well, he gave Old Red a shot, and he's all well."

Weeks passed and Old Red still lived outside the barber shop. I sometimes wondered if he ever noticed the dogs that came to the stores with families. Dogs often leaned out of car windows and barked at Old Red or just looked at him. Old Red didn't pay them any attention.

Jeremy continued to talk about the someone whom God would send to love Old Red.

One day we rode by the shop and Old Red was gone. I went in the barber shop and asked Larry where he was.

Larry started grinning as soon as I came in. "Where's the dog, Larry?" I got right to the point.

"Strangest thing happened yesterday. This lady brought her little boy in for a haircut. I didn't know them. New in this area. She asked about the dog. Her little boy had a fit over him. When I told her he didn't belong to anyone, she took him home with her."

"Larry, don't tease me."

"I'm not teasing. I'll give you her telephone number. I got it. She was going to take the dog to the vet for shots and a bath. Man, you should have seen Old Red sitting up in the front seat of that Buick. If I didn't know better, I'd say he was grinning. Happiest dog I've ever seen."

I walked out of the barber shop quickly. I didn't want Larry to see me crying.

# 13

## MORE THAN A SHELF

Hammering the nail into the wall, I suddenly remembered that since childhood I'd longed for a small shelf by my bed. I had even attempted to build one when I was about ten. Once I tried using a window ledge, but it didn't work. Finally, I'd given up on the idea.

But since my husband and I had papered our bedroom and I'd hung soft, new curtains, I'd started once again to think about having a small shelf by the side of my bed. Only a tiny space was available, about fourteen inches from the bed.

I wasn't sure I could make the shelf stay on the wall. Things had a habit of falling after I hung them. I mounted the small shelf while sitting on the bed, since there wasn't room to stand. As I put the board on the wall, I noticed that the wood was rough and uneven. "Why," I thought, "this is what I've imagined the Cross must have been like." I waited a few seconds to see if it would fall. Then I applied a little weight with one hand. The shelf stayed!

I lovingly selected items to put on my shelf. First, my old Bible— the one my mother had given me when I was nine. Then, almost painfully, I chose a few small books. There wasn't room for many. *The Christian's Secret of a Happy Life* by Hannah Whitall Smith was my first choice.

For bookends I used an antique candle holder with a bit of an old green candle in it, and on the other side of my "library" I placed a small wooden plaque. A little boy and girl looked at a distant rainbow. The printing said, "With God nothing is impossible." A wicker basket of ivy (that looked incredibly real) hung over the shelf. A few sprigs of real, miniature ivy in a minute golden bottle seemed just right. I added a picture of a quaint boy and girl carrying an old lantern. It fit perfectly over the shelf. The wording said, "Thy word is a lamp unto my feet, and a light unto my path" (Psalms 119:105, KJV).

Two decoupage prints of daisies about one inch by one inch glued to a piece of velvet ribbon, a plaque about fathers, and a pen and pencil for underlining completed my project.

I could hardly wait to see my family's reaction. After supper, we all went up to the bedroom so I could show everyone my finished project. My husband stared, silent and grim. I knew the look well.

"Mother," my sixteen-year-old daughter exclaimed, "that's not the place for a shelf. It's too crowded."

"What's it for?" one of the twins asked.

Fourteen-year-old Jennifer, who hates to hurt anyone's feelings, looked away silently.

My husband spoke: "If you turn over in bed, you'll bump your head. It just doesn't belong."

They filed out of the room, and I went to do the dishes, hoping my disappointment didn't show.

In bed that night I looked at it in the darkness. The moon illuminated the coarse grain of the shelf and outlined the books and small treasures. How could anyone not love my shelf? And when I woke up the next morning, even before I opened my eyes, I remembered to turn over so I could see my shelf the first thing. It hadn't fallen! Everything was intact. I didn't bump my head on it, either. I smiled at my shelf.

After my husband left for work and I'd gotten the four children off to school, I walked through our bedroom with a basket of dirty clothes. Quickly, I stole a glance at the shelf. The sun shone in through the window just then and seemed to light it up in a glorious way. It almost beckoned to me. I let the clothes slide to the floor, and all my family's criticism of my shelf seemed to slide away too. No matter what anyone had said, I liked it. It fulfilled some need in my life. I wasn't sure what. After crawling across the bed, I sat cross-legged, still in my gown, looking at my shelf with absolute joy. Happiness welled up inside me, so that tears brimmed my eyes. *Why am I so happy over this ridiculous shelf? No one likes it. I really should take it down.*

*I like it,* the Silent Voice spoke quietly to my heart.

Still crying, I began laughing. *Oh, Lord, it was You who put the desire in my heart for this shelf. I didn't know till this very moment —but it's much more than a shelf! It's my very own little altar. No one is supposed to like it or understand it. It's my place to meet You each day. Thank You for this idea.*

# 14

## A SMALL SATURDAY-NIGHT MIRACLE

I was exasperated with my sixteen-year-old daughter. Julie usually checked with me about her dating plans. She stood before me and insisted, "But I told you we were going to see the movie. Don't you remember?"

I'd been alarmed and sickened about the type of movies showing for quite some time. It had been years since I'd seen a movie and I left in tears because of the violence. It had been rated PG.

For the most part, our children were resigned to seeing very few movies. Julie and her boyfriend, Ricky, were content to stay home, cook a pizza, take walks, bowl, or go to ball games. Occasionally they went to a movie with Jerry's and my approval. I was more of a "stick in the mud" than Jerry.

Julie had never once given me any problems about her dating. She'd always been obedient and concerned about what I thought. I was grateful.

An ad in the movie section of the paper had caught my eye. The movie was rated PG, but the picture illustrating it suggested that much more awaited the viewer. The illustration was just short of being lewd. I made a mental note that the children wouldn't see that picture.

Now Julie stood before me telling me that this was the movie they planned to see. She hadn't seen the ad in the paper but said since it was rated PG it must be okay. She further insisted that she'd told me they were going and I'd said, "Okay." Maybe she had, and I'd been so busy I didn't pay attention to what she was saying. But Ricky was due in a few minutes and I simply could not give my permission for her to see the movie.

"Mother, I'll feel like a baby saying I can't go. There's nothing else on to see except Walt Disney."

"I can't give my permission, Julie. I'm sorry."

Quickly I prayed silently, "Lord, am I wrong? Am I being too strict? I feel so certain I'm right about this."

I seemed to feel an assurance from Him that the movie was unfit.
I sighed with relief. But my relief was short-lived. The Lord
seemed to add a P.S.: *Let her go.*

I argued with Him silently, thinking surely it had been the suggestion of Satan rather than the Lord. Finally I was convinced that
the Lord was telling me that the movie was unfit and to let Julie go.

Confused, I decided to put it in Jerry's hands. He had the final
say, anyway. I marched into the living room where he was reading
the sports page and handed him the movie section of the paper. I
pointed to the illustration that had caught my eye earlier. "This is
what Julie and Ricky are going to see tonight. What do you think?"
I would agree to whatever Jerry said, no matter how I felt. It was
something new I was learning about obedience. At first I couldn't
trust his decisions, but gradually I'd come to find out that the Lord
really does work in a wife's life through obedience to her husband.
Jerry had never taken advantage of my submission.

The doorbell rang before he could answer me, and Julie let Ricky
in. They both stood there looking at us. I encouraged Jerry (subtly
I thought) to say no.

Finally he spoke. "Julie, I'm going to let you go. I trust your and
Ricky's judgment."

Both their faces lit up.

I could have crawled under the sofa. I knew I was right. The
movie was unfit. I didn't understand what the Lord was doing or
what Jerry was doing. Was I the only one around here who had any
sense?

Just as Julie and Ricky started out the door, Jerry added, "Your
mother and I might go see the movie tomorrow."

Julie started to say something but decided to let well enough
alone. She waved good-bye. Ricky said good-bye. "Thanks," she
added.

I didn't really think we would go to the movie. For one thing,
Jerry seldom asked me to go to the movies since I'd walked out on
the last one we attended. I had sat in the lobby and cried and made
a small scene.

I'd been working on a writing assignment. I went back to it and
Jerry continued reading the paper. I sat for a moment looking at
my typewriter and thought, "Lord, I know I didn't misunderstand

You. You wanted them to go and yet that movie's going to be bad. I know it. I don't understand what You're doing. But I'm going to trust You. Please go with them and protect them."

I had two choices. To brood about the whole thing and pick a fight with Jerry or really trust the Lord, like I'd prayed. I sighed and resumed my work.

I became so absorbed in my writing that I almost forgot completely about Julie and Ricky. About forty-five minutes passed. I was hunched over the typewriter reading something that I'd become completely wrapped up in. I became aware of someone standing in the kitchen looking down into the den. I looked up. There stood Julie and Ricky. Julie was positively beaming! Ricky sort of looked around like he was studying the wallpaper, but he looked mildly pleased. I just stared at them trying to figure out what had happened. Julie explained before I could ask. "In the first fifteen minutes of the movie, Ricky said we had to leave. I didn't want to at first because we couldn't get our money back. I thought maybe it would get—better, you know. But he said it was going to get worse. We left. Walked out. We're going to fix a pizza, okay?"

"Okay," I smiled, knowing that I mustn't say too much right now. Joy flooded through me. The Lord had been right after all. How proud I was of Ricky for his judgment. He seemed to grow ten feet tall standing right there in my kitchen looking at the wallpaper. He was more special than I'd realized. I was grateful that Julie had selected someone like him to date.

Ricky went to read part of the paper with Jerry, and Julie fixed the pizza. I sat looking at her. She turned around and said, "Ricky's got good judgment."

I nodded.

"You have too, Mama," she added.

I resumed my typing thinking, so had my Father.

AUTHOR'S NOTE: Julie and Ricky were married two years later.

# 15

## LISTENING

I'd just seen the girls off to school and said good-bye to my husband when I sat down with a cup of coffee at my kitchen table for a few quiet moments. I was speaking to a group of women at nine thirty, so I knew I couldn't sit for long. The boys were upstairs dressing and had to be prodded to hurry.

Suddenly the front door swung open, and Jerry faced me silently. He'd never come home like this, in the twenty years that we'd been married. I knew he was on a tight schedule and that the school traffic had already made coming back quite time-consuming.

"I have to tell you something," he said quietly.

"What in the world," I thought, "would he come back home for? He could have called me when he got to work." My mind was a total blank.

"Wingate is dead. She's just been hit. I can't move her out of the road because of the traffic. I wanted you to know before you had to drive by and see her. I know you're leaving in a little while. It happened after the girls left. You'll have to tell the boys. I have to go."

Wingate, our eleven-year-old cat, had never ventured from our yard. She was terrified of the street and cars. She didn't like most people, and often seemed merely to put up with us. Lately, we'd noticed signs of senility. She'd been acting like a kitten again, developing new habits. The streets were completely foreign to her, and she'd picked the busiest hour to dart across.

Quickly I thought, "I simply cannot handle this now, not when I'm about to speak." I asked, "Are you certain she's . . . dead?"

"Yes, her . . . head is almost gone."

I nodded. "Thank you for coming back."

Jerry kissed me again and left.

I continued sitting at the table. I couldn't think of what to do. Briefly I remembered the three other cats we'd lost. Once I cried for two days. I'd even cried when a neighbor's cat had been killed.

And it wasn't unusual for me to shed tears over a dead cat on the highway.

Wingate gone? So quick? Just this morning I'd watched one of the children let her out the front door. She'd stood in the doorway for a moment glaring at the bright sunlight. Then she padded softly down the steps. I couldn't remember which child had let her out. Just as well. I looked at her bowl of milk, half empty. "She's out there in the street, and I'm going to have to drive by her when I go to speak. I can't cancel this late. Dear Lord, how will I do it? Give me Your strength. I have none of my own. I can't cry now. Keep the tears away."

I told Jon and Jeremy about Wingate and they nodded their heads quietly. A friend of theirs came over to wait for the school bus with them and told us that the car that killed our cat had tried very hard to stop and miss her. I was grateful to know that. It helped some.

A blessed numbness seemed to fill my heart and somewhat like Scarlett O'Hara I rationalized, "well, I'll think about this whole thing tomorrow. Any time but now."

I dressed for the meeting and had a few extra minutes. I looked through my Bible for some scripture to get me through the ordeal of seeing Wingate without a head in the middle of the road.

A scripture popped into my mind, a familiar one. "I can do all things through Christ which strengtheneth me" (Philippians 4:13, KJV). It seemed appropriate for the situation. Another thought came into my mind. "You are a Christian. God will help you do *anything*. You can go out there and get Wingate up. Surely you can do that. The traffic has died down now. You can do anything with the Lord's help. You have time. Go on."

I started out the door feeling that I could do it, and even as I backed the car out, I thought, I can do this with His help.

I've often heard it taught that Satan can quote scripture, but I don't know that I'd ever experienced it. Suddenly I saw the cars going around the object in the highway. "Oh, God, can I do it?"

With sudden clarity the answer came from Him. "You don't have to do this. It's not necessary. I didn't tell you to stop and pick up Wingate. Just don't even look at her. Keep your eyes on Me and drive right by. Listen to Me."

As I approached our cat, the traffic had died down quite a bit and I looked away quickly. But briefly I saw that her body was perfectly intact, curled like she was sleeping. The head—simply was not there. I noticed that she still had on her collar. I wondered if her name tag were still attached to the collar. I wanted it, but I had my traveling instructions. As I drove I thought about a song that says to turn your eyes upon Jesus. Look fully in His face and the things of the world will grow strangely dim in the light of His wonder and grace. I hummed the song as I drove past our beloved cat in the road. I didn't feel anything except gratitude. God was protecting me with His banner of love. I couldn't grieve. I didn't understand it, but I accepted it.

I shared my testimony at the meeting and that day I ended it differently. I told the group about Wingate and the way the Lord had reminded me to look at Him, not the situation. Some cat lovers in the group cried openly. I still couldn't shed tears. It wasn't a matter of holding them back. There simply weren't any.

Coming back home a few hours later, Wingate was still in the road. She'd been hit several more times. Satan made another suggestion. "Why don't you get the cat out of the road now before your children and husband have to see her like that? Jerry will have to scoop her up. What an ordeal for him. You know he loved her too. Go ahead; get her up. The Lord will help you."

"Father . . ." I began.

"Don't do it. I told you not to do it. Keep your eyes on Me. Listen carefully to Me." I drove past without looking at Wingate.

Sitting in my living room, I thought about my family having to see Wingate. I didn't want that. As I sat staring out the window, still feeling no deep grief, the garbage truck came rumbling down the street. They were late today, usually came in the morning.

"Move," His voice prompted me.

Suddenly I jumped up and ran outside and flagged down the truck. "Do you pick up dead animals?" I asked the young boy hanging on to the side of the truck.

"No, ma'am, we're not allowed to."

"Oh," I said. "I thought maybe you could get my cat for me."

"We can't. Sorry."

The driver of the truck, an older man, stuck his head out the window. "Where's the animal? Could you put it on the truck?"

"Oh, no. I can't even look at my cat. She's right out there in the highway and I thought maybe you all could . . ."

"We'll get her for you."

I didn't question why he was making an exception. "Oh, thank you. Wait a minute." I ran back into the house and got a plastic bag and the dustpan and a dollar bill (all I had). I handed the sack and dustpan to the young man. "Just throw the dustpan away."

He nodded. I handed him the dollar. "Thank you," I smiled.

He sort of smiled, and they drove off.

I went in the house and didn't look out the window anymore. I still didn't feel grief or remorse that the trash man was picking up our cat. I didn't want Jerry to have to do it.

How good God is when we listen to Him, I thought. We remembered Wingate in many happy conversations. I never cried.

It was months later that a neighbor came to my door. He handed me something. "Thought you might want this. I was walking the other day, getting my exercise, and saw something shining in the sun. I don't know how I never saw it in all those weeks, but the sun really hit on it just right. Made it shine like a light." He handed me the small, round disk. I looked down in my hand and saw Wingate's name tag. Her name and our address were legible. There was a nick in it from the impact.

I closed my hand over the disk and thought, "You don't forget the smallest detail, do you, Lord? Thank you."

"Thank you, thank you so much," I said to the neighbor. "I know it's a miracle that you found it."

He nodded and left.

Every time I see the disk, which I keep on my desk, I'm reminded of the importance of listening to the Lord before I take any action. I have a bad habit of driving head on into situations, like a charging bull. I'm trying to learn to keep my eyes on Jesus and listen to Him alone.

# *16*

## LET ME COUNT THE WAYS*

Since high school I have loved romantic, sentimental declarations of love. I once kept a scrapbook of different ways great poets said, "I love you." I can still recall as a fifteen-year-old discovering one of Shakespeare's love sonnets and promptly memorizing it. Enthralled with "Annabel Lee," I taught it to my first child by the time she entered kindergarten. She came home and asked why I'd never read her any good stuff, like "Jack and Jill."

While still single, I gazed openly at married couples and thought, "They must spend hours each day talking about the depth and height and breadth of their love." I could hardly wait to do that. I envisioned that once my beloved and I were joined together by marriage, we would wander through life hand in hand, marveling over our profound love. Flowers would bloom wherever we trod—just like in Walt Disney movies.

I also imagined that we'd hardly notice such mundane things as what we ate. We'd be so engrossed in expressing our love to each other that food would be of little importance. And I would discover love notes from my husband hidden around the house. He'd call from work just to say, "I love you." At the end of the day, I'd hear his car in the driveway and within two seconds my husband would burst through the door and gather me in his arms and tell me of seven new ways he loved me. Probably some day he'd bring me something like a book of love poems he'd found on his lunch hour or a single red rose.

I have now been married for almost nineteen years. Jerry and I have four children, and I'm forty-one years old. My husband has never called in the middle of the day to declare his love for me. He doesn't even like to talk on the phone. I did find a note Scotch-taped on the refrigerator once, but it could hardly be classified as a love note. It said, "There's something rotten in here."

* From *Marriage and Family Living*, September 1977. Reprinted with the permission of *Marriage and Family Living* magazine.

It's often quite late when I hear his car in the driveway. (It's still the sweetest sound of the day.) Our two teenaged daughters call out, "Daddy's home," and make their way to the front door. The nine-year-old twin boys push and shove each other trying to get to the door first. Three cats move cautiously in that direction.

The door opens, and Jerry's home. All the children talk at once. The boys jump up and down while they talk. The cats meow frantically.

In the background, I put ice in the glasses, pour tea, and check the biscuits in the oven, admiring my husband from afar. Finally he comes into the kitchen and peeks under lids on the stove. (I learned while still a bride that food would be of prime importance.)

However, I don't give up on dreams easily. Sometimes I imagine Jerry will announce firmly, "Quiet. Everyone leave. Cats too. I want to be alone with my wife." As everyone melts into the background, my husband throws his briefcase aside, crushes me in his arms while humming, "Have I Told You Lately That I Love You?"

The other day while scrubbing the bathtub and mumbling to myself, "How do I love thee? Let me count the ways," I stopped and remembered something I'd read about love. I couldn't recall it exactly, so I grabbed a towel, wiped off my hands, and got my Bible. Sitting back down on the bathroom floor by the half-scrubbed tub, I read, "Love is very patient and kind, never jealous or envious, never boastful or proud, never haughty or selfish or rude. Love does not demand its own way. It is not irritable or touchy. It does not hold grudges and will hardly even notice when others do it wrong. It is never glad about injustice, but rejoices whenever truth wins out. If you love someone you will be loyal to him no matter what the cost. You will always believe in him, always expect the best of him, and always stand your ground in defending him" (I Corinthians 13:4-7, TLB).

Something occurred to me with rapid-fire speed and unmistakable clarity. Even though my husband didn't say it in romantic, hearts-and-flowers poems or speeches, he'd been telling me for nineteen years that he loved me! He said it in clever, unromantic ways.

Why, just yesterday Jerry had come in and flashed a giant package of zinnia seeds in my face. I'd asked him to plant some flowers for me in his vegetable garden. My flower seeds never come up. Jerry has a way with growing things. He had complained, "I don't have much room in my garden as it is. I need all that space for vegetables."

Nevertheless, the first thing he planted was the giant package of zinnia seeds. A few weeks later he proudly showed me where all the baby plants had come up in his garden-to-be.

Because I love animals, domestic and wild, with an unreasonable love, Jerry once took a wild rabbit our dog had caught to the vet at my insistence. And through the years he's allowed me to bring home stray cats or dogs. Once he even went out into the snow late at night to help me search for a sick dog I'd seen by the roadside. Oh, he complained that it was a silly thing to do, but he drove slowly down a street calling, "Here, dog."

My husband isn't shy at all. He meets people much easier than I do. But when I wrote a book about us, he about flipped. "You can't publish this," he said, "it's too personal." Weeks later, despite his feelings, he told me, "Send your book off. It's good."

Right after our twins were born, I went shopping. It was a breathtakingly pastel spring, and I was small once again. I brought home two outfits to see which one Jerry liked the best. One was a sensible, nice dress. The other a fantastic pink dress with a matching coat. I felt like a teenager in her first formal in it, but the cost was way out of line for us. I told Jerry how much each dress cost and asked, "Which one do you like the best?"

He didn't look at the dresses but at my face. He answered without hesitation, "Get the pink number."

When we were expecting our first child I had the usual cravings —pickles and ice cream. I also had an unusual craving right before the baby arrived. Jerry and I made a mad dash to the dime store one evening just before it closed. A saleswoman approached us: "May I help you?"

"We want a coloring book and colors," I answered with excitement.

"What age child are you buying for?" she replied.

"Oh, it's for my wife," Jerry answered proudly. "She wants to color and smell crayons."

Without further comment she and other saleswomen watched as

I selected a ballerina coloring book and a box of sixty-four Jumbo colors.

We have two cars. A nice, normal station wagon and another car which we refer to as the blue goose. The goose has a multitude of problems, including no heater. One morning Jerry announced, "I'll take the goose to work today." The temperature was in the low teens and it's an hour's drive to his office. I had a few errands to run that day, but I drove in warmth. And at that time I didn't even think that driving the goose to work was his quiet way of saying, "I love you."

Oh, Elizabeth Browning, I wish you could know how much my husband loves me! Let me count the ways!

1. He has proper insurance and a will.
2. He shampoos the carpets and papers walls.
3. He builds shelves.
4. He cuts the grass each week with a push mower.
5. He straightens out the checkbook when I think I've ruined it forever.
6. He saves me hot water at night by taking a skimpy bath.
7. He tells me when I need new tires on the car.
8. He goes downstairs at night to get me a drink of water.
9. He's nice to *all* my friends, even if they're strange (i.e., writers).
10. He believes me.
11. He encourages me.
12. He prays with me.
13. He listens to me.
14. He doesn't say, "I told you so," when I'm wrong.

And in his steadfast, unique way tells me each day, *"Hey, I love you!"*

# *17*

## THE CHRISTMAS GIFT

Leaning on Jesus came more natural as a child. I was more aware that I needed someone to lean on. I remember one Christmas that I leaned heavily on Him and He met my deepest need. I didn't have to work at leaning then.

I watched from inside the house as my mother lugged a bucket of coal up the back steps. There were seventeen steps, and she would bring up three loads of coal. She'd smile at me when she passed the window. Many times I'd shout through the window, "Let me help!"

Her answer remained the same. "No. You stay inside where it's warm, Mannie. This only takes a minute. Besides, there's only one bucket." I must have been about nine years old.

*You shouldn't have to do this, Mama. You've already worked all day in an office. I know you're tired.*

Sometimes I wouldn't watch out the window. I'd busy myself in some other part of the house until I knew the coal for the next day had been brought up. Often I imagined we had central heat and there was no need for coal. Or I'd think about my friends who had fathers who could bring coal in. My own father had died before I was two.

Even though my mother had to go to work each day, and I missed not having a father, there was a lot of happiness in our life together in the small three-room apartment.

As I grew older I'd bring up the coal some days before my mother got home from work. It was terribly heavy, and I could never seem to get an adequate supply. I wanted to figure out some way to make things better for her.

Unexpectedly, when I was about thirteen, I got a job wrapping Christmas gifts at a local department store. On busy days I worked from nine in the morning until seven thirty in the evening. Although I was young and inexperienced, I worked quickly. I earned twenty-three cents an hour. I was to get paid just before Christmas.

I wanted to get my mother something special for Christmas—something to make life easier for her. After work one evening I was window-shopping. I saw what my mother must have. A dark-haired mannequin modeled it. She had a radiant smile, and there were no tired lines on her face. She appeared pampered and relaxed in the moss green satin lounging pajamas and short matching robe. She was about the size of my mother, I thought. I strained to see the price tag, turning my head almost upside down.

$25.95.

I had no idea if I would earn that much money. And if I did, someone else might buy the beautiful set before I did. "Dear God," I prayed, looking intently at the pajamas, "hold them for me. Don't let anyone buy them, and let me make twenty-five, ninety-five, at least."

Many evenings after work I went by the dress shop and stood in front of the window looking at the pajamas. I would look at them and smile with deep satisfaction. It was always a relief to see that they were still there.

Two nights before Christmas, I got paid. I poured the money out of my pay envelope and counted it. *Twenty-seven dollars and thirteen cents!* I had more than enough. I ran to the store with the money in my pocket. I entered out of breath and said to the saleslady, "I want to buy the beautiful pajamas set in the window. It's twenty-five, ninety-five."

The saleswoman knew me and my mother. She smiled warmly, but suggested, "Marion, don't you think your mother would rather have something more—practical?"

I shook my head. I didn't even understand her subtle, kind suggestion. Nothing on earth could have changed my mind. Those pajamas were for my mother. God had kept everyone from buying them, and I had the money to pay for them. I watched almost breathlessly as the woman took the pajamas and robe out of the window. While she got a box, I reached out and touched the soft satin. It was an exquisite moment, and I thought I might cry. She wrapped the gift in soft tissue paper first, then in Christmas paper.

Finally, with the large package under my arm, I headed home. I put my gift under the tree, wondering how I'd wait until Christmas morning.

When it dawned, I couldn't open any of my gifts until my mother opened hers. I watched with a pounding heart.

She pulled back the tissue paper and her mouth formed a silent O. She touched the pajamas with one finger—then held up the robe. She looked at me and said, "Oh, Mannie! It's the most beautiful thing I've ever seen. I don't know how you managed it, but I love it!"

I smiled and said, "Put it on, Mama."

She did and cooked breakfast in the outfit. All morning and into the afternoon she told me how much she loved the gift. I knew she would. She showed it to everyone who came by.

Through the years, even after they'd fallen apart, my mother would still tell people about those green satin pajamas.

I reasoned that somehow my gift had made up for her having to bring in coal, build fires, and go to work—walking at that. Each evening my mother would put on her satin pajamas and we'd sit by the fire listening to the radio, reading or talking.

As a child, I never realized that I should have gotten her a sweater or boots. No one could have talked me into it. The green satin pajamas seemed to transform us into another world, just like I knew they would.

This story could end there, but there seems to be more. After I had children of my own my mother was visiting with us one Christmas. Despite the joy of the season, I was a bit weary. It seemed like I'd been tired for months—maybe years. I'd finally come to realize that motherhood is a full-time, often mundane job, *every day*. The demands of raising a family had begun to show on my face and in my attitude.

The children squealed and tore into their presents. We were knee-deep in paper, which I'd later have to clean up. Just then my mother handed me a present. "Merry Christmas, Mannie," she said softly.

She hadn't opened her gifts. She watched me as I carefully opened the large, golden package. I folded back pink tissue paper and caught my breath. Slowly I lifted out the most beautiful, elegant pink-and-gold silk lounging robe I'd ever seen. I ran my hand over the gold-embossed design. "Ohhh," was all I could manage for a few moments. Then I said, "I can't believe it's for me. It's not something a mother would wear." I looked down at my worn flannel robe through a blur of tears.

"Put it on," my mother urged.

As I threw off the old robe, it seemed that I shed discouragement and weariness too! I stood up joyfully wrapped in the lovely silk robe, knowing fully how Cinderella must have felt.

"Hey," one of the children said, "look at Mama. She's pretty." Everyone looked at me. My husband smiled.

Standing there that Christmas morning in the elegant robe, I suddenly remembered back through the years and recalled those green satin pajamas. I looked at my mother. I believe she remembered them too. She must have, to have known how desperately I needed that robe. There was no need to say anything. We both understood the gifts too well.

# 18

## THE PRAYER TRUCK

The earliest leaning experience I ever had must have occurred when I was about six or seven. To my knowledge it was the first time I asked God for the impossible. Logic could prove that my prayer would have been answered even if I hadn't prayed it. Perhaps it could be proved that I didn't understand the mechanics of prayer. Maybe I wasn't even old enough to pray with faith. Nevertheless, I knew that something quite wonderful had happened in my life. I didn't know then to call it leaning on Jesus, though.

I had ordered a doll from the Sears catalog. From the day my mother mailed the order, I planted myself on our front steps to wait for the mailman. I'd been looking in the catalog for a long time at this particular doll. I'd ordered small things before, like rings from cereal boxes, but this was really something big. Each morning when the mailman came across our yard carrying his worn mail satchel, I'd think, "I'll bet he's got my doll today."

Three days passed. The waiting seemed unbearable. "Today will be the day," I decided. The mailman saw me sitting on the steps. We were friends. He ended my suspense quickly, "Nothing today for you, Marion."

I nodded my head and disappointment surged through me like waves of nausea. I smiled at the postman and pretended to look through the letters he handed me. When he was out of sight I started to cry.

Just then a bird called out loudly and startled me. I looked up at the bird and, when I did, the vast blue sky seemed to overwhelm me. Still looking up into the heavens, I decided to ask God for the impossible. "Please, God, please send me my doll today. I've waited so long. I don't know how You can get her here today. The mail's already come and she wasn't in it, but just please do it somehow."

I sat there stunned at my foolish prayer, yet overjoyed with my sudden spurt of faith. I smiled, relaxed, and continued watching the cars that passed by our house. I thought about the doll. I imagined holding her and changing her diapers.

I leaned forward to watch a big, brown truck come slowly down the street. The driver stopped the truck in front of our house and got out. He wore a brown uniform of some kind and carried something under his arm.

He came across our yard and asked, "Are you Marion Bond?"

"Yes, sir," I answered, my eyes fixed on the small package under his arm.

"I have something for you. Sign here, please."

I printed my name so hard that I broke the pencil point.

"That's okay." He smiled and handed me another pencil. "Bye." Then he handed me the package. Up in the corner it said "Sears." My heart beat rapidly. I sat the box in my lap and looked down at it. I knew my doll was inside, but I looked at the box for a long time. I turned it over and over and over. I was thrilled beyond words to have my doll, but I was even more amazed at the immediate answer to my foolish prayer. God had done the impossible.

I looked up at the sky again and said, "Thank you, God. I won't forget this." Before I unwrapped the package, I glanced at the truck just as it turned the corner. I got a quick glimpse of three large golden letters on the side of the truck: UPS. There was more writing, but I couldn't read it. I didn't know what the U stood for, but I grinned suddenly. PS must mean Prayer Special. A Prayer Truck sent by God had brought my doll! She was very special.

Thirty-three years have passed since the United Parcel Service man delivered my package. A routine delivery for him was a big miracle in my life. And I'm convinced that I must once again live with the foolish faith of a child who leans with absolute trust on the Father, Who loves to give His children good gifts.

# 19

## HONESTY

When I speak to groups of women, almost no one appears to have a problem of any kind. Everyone is smiling and confident-looking. Nevertheless, I have learned that beneath those self-assured-appearing women often are desperate mothers and wives. They are wearing a mask of make-believe. I know about masks. I wore one for years.

Often when I speak, women come by and make appropriate well-meaning comments: "I enjoyed your talk, it was inspirational"; "Thank you for coming"; even, "I could identify with you." They smile and move along. But there are always a few who rip off the masks, and I pray hurriedly that I'll say the right things to them.

Comments such as: "I'm a minister's wife and I've never said this, but I don't like one of my children"; "I don't like myself—there's something I can't forgive myself for . . ."; "I'm terrified every day of my life. No one knows . . ." I always admire these women. Honesty can be extremely painful. Sometimes women have just sat quietly and waited until most everyone else was gone; then they came over and cried without speaking.

Just before Christmas I spoke to a church group in the home of one of the members. The home was elegant, yet warm and comfortable. As the women arrived, I couldn't help but notice how young and carefree most of them were. It was a small group, perhaps fifteen. They were all close friends. The women seemed happy, content, and charming, like the elegant-looking women who modeled in magazines with well-behaved children. They were dressed casually, yet spiffily.

I wondered, watching them, if they could identify with any of the things I'd be sharing. I'd never come up against such a completely "all-together"-looking group of women. Their hair and makeup reflected excellent taste. I thought, "They're probably just as calm on the inside as on the outside."

Most of them had their Bibles, and I heard snatches of what the

Lord was doing in their lives. We ate a beautiful lunch out of china plates. Everywhere I looked I saw a smile. No one even looked tired. They'd probably left spotless homes, or had maids cleaning them. My own house had been left in a mess.

The bathroom was so lovely, creative, and sparkling that I decided no one with a bathroom like that could possibly have any problems in her life. I felt sure all the women had bathrooms like the one of the hostess.

"Lord, what am I doing here? They all appear to have the world by the tail. I wish I could just leave without speaking."

As we sat around chatting before I was introduced, I kept noticing a young woman. I had seen her when she came in. Everyone turned to greet her when she bounced in breathlessly. She wore a beige satin blouse that would have looked tacky on me. On her it was stunning. Her straight, simple haircut bobbed about as she spoke. She was probably one of the first women to push sunglasses up on her head and look great in them. Her jewelry blended perfectly with her outfit. She could have been a model. She moved gracefully, and people seemed to like to listen to her. Her voice wasn't loud, but it carried well. She spoke about her Christmas decorations for the holidays. "I'm having real garlands made for the stairway and mantel, and I want to go back to that little shop and get more of the adorable handmade burlap tree ornaments. Don't you just love to decorate for Christmas?"

I'd been looking at a box of shiny balls for $5.98 at the drugstore, wondering if that was too much to spend. She continued, "I'm having red velvet dresses made for my girls to wear when company comes by, and I believe I'm going to splurge and get some Christmas dishes this year. I've always wanted some." She continued talking, not in a loud way, but I heard. I liked listening to her. Others seemed to also. She spoke fondly of her husband and their two daughters.

In my mind I could see them all as they appeared in the doorway of their beautifully decorated home and greeted guests who popped in unannounced. This woman and her family were always ready for company—the house immaculate. It probably sat way back from the street and glowed softly.

At the business meeting before I spoke, this woman seemed to have the answer to every problem. She made recommendations and came up with clever ideas. She volunteered to make a tablecloth for their Christmas party. Everyone ohhed and ahhed at how artistic and clever she was with her decorative ideas.

Finally, the hostess introduced me. The lovely women smiled throughout my testimony. I couldn't imagine that any of them identified with the things I shared. What could they know of desperation and depression.

I forgot about the lovely, talented woman in the satin blouse and concentrated on a quiet little woman who seemed never to smile. How had I missed her? My testimony was probably just for her. Her expression never changed.

Afterward people came up and said appropriate things. I was just about to leave when the young woman in the satin blouse was suddenly standing before me. She smiled, so I expected a polite comment. The others were now in the kitchen cleaning up. Without warning her face crumpled like tissue paper and she sobbed: "I wasn't coming today. But at the last minute, I did. I'm a phony—scared to death. I don't love my husband. He hates me. I scream at my children all day, and I wake up dreading each new day. I don't want to live anymore like this." The tears flowed down her face and plopped onto her blouse. She twisted her gold beads. "My marriage is about over. We're going to get a divorce after Christmas. Only a miracle could save it." She made an effort to regain her composure. Her mascara streamed down her face and she found a tissue in her purse. It had gold roses on it and matched her blouse.

"Father, what do I do?" I prayed quickly as I listened and hurt with her. She stopped finally and looked down, adding softly, "No one knows I'm having problems. They think everything is wonderful at my house . . ."

I can't recall the exact words, but I said, "Carol,* did you grow up believing that the Lord helps those who help themselves?"

She nodded and almost whispered, "Doesn't He?"

I shook my head. "Not according to the Bible. He helps desperate, broken people. Are you there yet?"

She nodded her head. "I can't pretend anymore."

* Real name not used.

The others were coming back into the den. Carol looked uncomfortable only for a moment. Then she smiled her radiant smile. She pulled the large sunglasses down over her red eyes, and when she spoke the light tone was back in her voice.

I said in hushed tones, "Be honest with Jesus, Carol. Stop pretending. Admit all your inadequacies and fears. Tell Him about your inability to love. Throw yourself on Him. He'll save your marriage. He's just waiting for you to stop trying so hard. Give up, Carol. Please, give up. You'll never make it this way. He's just waiting for you to depend on Him."

She hugged me quickly and walked away. She had become quiet but still smiled. She spoke briefly to others as she left. I watched out the window as she walked to her car. She got in her sleek beige car that matched her blouse and drove away.

*Father, help her lean. Don't let anything keep her from leaning. Thank You for her honesty here today. And, Father, forgive me for judging people—by bathrooms and blouses and Christmas decorations.*

# 20

## RECEIVING

Our house guest and her son had finally arrived to spend a week with us. We'd never met. A few years ago she'd read something I'd written, and when she wrote to me we began corresponding. I knew she was a Christian but with many troubles. The problem seemed to center around her marriage.

I hadn't been sure I'd recognize Thelma and her son, David,* as I met the early morning bus, but I did. I knew them the moment they stepped from the bus. We made polite conversation driving to our house. Jon and Jeremy did a lot to keep the conversation going. I tried to get them to stop asking questions, as I was certain our visitors were worn out from their fourteen-hour bus trip. Thelma had asked almost cautiously through letters if she could visit.

At home, our boys hit it off great. They were loud and in constant motion, but happy. Thelma always wanted to talk about the Lord, read Christian books, watch Christian television, or go to a meeting that centered on Jesus.

On the third day of her visit, I began to realize that Thelma had a very deep-seated problem. I started trying to avoid conversations of a deep nature, and keep our talks light. I just didn't feel equipped to handle her situation. I suggested several counselors that I knew of, but she'd just shake her head. I remembered that before she came she said she thought she could find some spiritual answers at my house. Maybe she'd thought my house would be some kind of sanctuary, but it was far from that. With my four children, her one, and the constantly ringing telephone, and all the meals that had to be prepared and the daily loads of washing, it was like a three-ring circus. Jerry remained extremely polite and friendly, but I caught the look in his eyes: "What have you gotten yourself into?"

Mostly, Thelma liked to talk at night, when the children were in

* Names have been changed.

bed. I go to bed about ten myself, and can hardly stay awake past that time, especially with the active days I'd been having. I'd been excusing myself and going to bed at my regular time.

But on that third night, Thelma sat at the kitchen table with her Bible. She wore a very grave expression. She didn't even try to fake a smile. She was a very logical, matter-of-fact person, not emotional like me. I didn't really know how to talk to her. I'd said almost everything I knew to say. What can you tell a woman whose husband is an alcoholic? I couldn't imagine what it would be like to have Jerry steal grocery money that I'd earned. What would it be like to be afraid of him or watch my children fear their father? We'd had disagreements. I'd been angry enough to leave (for a while) but I never had done it. I wasn't afraid of him. I loved his marvelous wit, quiet manner, and blue eyes that could look grave or fill with exploding humor.

My heart seemed frozen with fear. I didn't know what to tell Thelma. Why was she so determined that I had answers for her? If her problem was screaming at her children or depression, I might be able to help her. But her problem was beyond me. I'd talked and shared till I was exhausted.

I started to pass by her on my way to bed. "Wow, it's after ten thirty already," I yawned.

She looked at me silently. Her look cut into my heart so that I nearly flinched. The Lord seemed to speak to me, as sleepy as I was: "I sent her here. If you keep running from her, you can't fit into what I have planned. Stop running. I know you don't know what to do. Trust me."

I longed to crawl into bed and cover up my head and forget the problems of Thelma and her husband. I had to decide whether to obey the Lord or go on my feelings. I was desperately tired with no answers. Maybe it hadn't been the Lord speaking to me after all. Anyway, if I stayed up and talked some more, I was afraid that I'd tell Thelma to leave Sammy.

Suddenly she started crying. She wasn't the type to cry. She was extremely efficient and so logical that I almost felt uncomfortable around her. She read instructions carefully (every word) and followed them to the letter. I almost never read instructions. "It doesn't work," she sobbed.

"What doesn't work?" I asked, still standing. If I sat down, that would mean that we were going to talk some more.

"This book." She lifted the Bible and continued crying.

New energy seemed to surge through me, and I knew that it had been the Lord talking to me in His soft, gentle voice. "Yes it does," I practically screamed. I lowered my voice, "Do you believe all of it?"

"Yes," she answered simply.

I sat down at the table with her and told the Lord silently, "I'm sorry for running. For not trusting You, for letting fear rule my decision. My time is Your time. Your energy is sufficient. I'm willing to sit here all night if that's what it takes, but You must understand—I don't have any answers."

"Good," the Lord seemed to answer quickly. Thelma still cried and said, "It says that if you ask for something, you can have it. I have asked and asked for Sammy to be saved. Why hasn't God saved him?"

Before I could give her any kind of answer, the Lord silenced my mouth. Just listen for a while. And Thelma didn't really stop long enough for me to speak. Relieved, I relaxed. Thelma talked openly about Sammy. No one where they lived knew about the drinking problem. She was helping him hide his secret. It became obvious that Thelma hated Sammy. I began to hate him too. "Marriage is not to be run away from because it gets difficult. That's what this book says." She pointed to the Bible. Boy, did she ever believe in going by instructions!

I nodded.

"So there has to be a way. Why can't I find it?" She looked right at me and said, "I'm about six months, at the longest, away from a complete nervous breakdown."

"I don't know what to do, Lord," I prayed silently. "She needs some good counseling." Immediately the thought that the Holy Spirit is a counselor popped into my mind. I listened to Thelma for a long time. I felt so relaxed and wide awake that I knew the Lord was at the table with us and that He was at work. There was no pressure on me whatsoever. I didn't know what to do, and that was okay. He'd have to tell me, or I'd just sit there and doodle on the tablecloth with my finger.

I can't recall our conversation exactly, except that I know I said so very little. I seemed to know when to speak, with amazing clarity, so that it was as though someone was giving me cues from off stage. The whole thing seemed remarkably simple. One of the questions I asked Thelma was, "Do you need Sammy?"

"No," she shot back at me. "I don't need him. I make a good salary, and I'd have a better life without him."

Next question: "Do you think that might be why he moved to the sofa to sleep six months ago?"

She looked startled and said softly, "Could be."

"How long has it been since you told him something good about himself?"

She shook her head and looked down.

"How long has he been drinking?" (I didn't know where the questions were leading.)

She began to calculate and came up with the answer, "Why . . . since, yes! Since I became a Christian . . . and the drinking became worse when I received the baptism of the Holy Spirit."

Next question: "Don't you think that falling in love with Jesus could seem to a nonbelieving husband almost like you loved someone else—another man?"

She looked at me, and I didn't know what to expect. It wasn't my question.

Thelma thought for a moment. I could almost see the logic spinning around in her mind. Then she answered, "Yes. Of course. That makes sense. It's logical."

I was beginning to like Sammy a little bit. "Sammy is created in God's image. God loves him so much, but he doesn't know it. And Sammy's saved. Jesus died for him. He just hasn't received his salvation yet. He doesn't know it's for him. He's got to be loved and prayed out of Satan's camp. Sammy's miserable."

She smiled slowly, almost cautiously. "Sammy is wonderful at fixing things. When my girlfriend moved across town, he took a day off from work and moved her, and then fixed some things that were broken in her apartment. He wanted to do it." Her voice became soft, almost happy. Her facial expression was gentle.

I felt Satan lunge in our midst. "But," she said with the panic in her voice again, "I have given myself, my will to the Lord. I've done all I know to do. Nothing is different. So many bad things happen each day. Where is God?"

"Lord," I bellowed silently, "what do I say?"

"Thelma, when you gave all of yourself to the Lord, it included your past, present, and future. You trusted Him for everything, each future problem, right?"

"Yes. Why doesn't He help?"

"When the future becomes the present, you have to remember your commitment. Say, 'Well, here's this problem again, Lord. I can't handle it. You do it. Remember, I gave this to You.' Do you do that?"

Her mouth opened silently and she said, "No, I don't do that. I just try harder myself. I love the logic of what you just said."

I didn't even really understand it completely. It was very difficult, or incredibly simple. I wasn't sure which. Actually, it didn't even sound so great to me, but then I'm not logical. I became aware that Thelma wanted me to pray with her. Yet, I didn't. "What's wrong with me, Lord?"

"Don't pray just yet," He seemed to instruct me.

"Okay."

"Stay relaxed and lean on Me. Don't mess this up."

I doodled with my finger some more on the tablecloth and remained silent. The silence was comfortable, almost comforting.

Next question. "Thelma, have you ever received Sammy?"

"Receive? What do you mean?"

"You know, when you get married, the minister says, 'Do you take this man to be your husband?' Did you take Sammy—receive him—just like he was—the way God receives us like we are when we come to Him?"

She sat up straight and clapped her hands together, and over and over she said the word "receive."

While she kept saying, "Receive," I looked at the clock and rejoiced that it was eleven twenty-five and I wasn't a bit sleepy. I hadn't been up this late in ages.

Suddenly Thelma held her head in her hands and moaned, "There's so much I have to do. So much! Where do I begin? I have to apologize, love, praise, receive . . ."

Logical Thelma, she would make a list. I didn't know what to tell her.

"I can't do everything at once. There's too much to do, at least ten things."

I remained silent, hoping I wouldn't have to name the things. She was way ahead of me.

"I know. I'll start with number one."

I could go along with that. I couldn't wait to see what it would be.

"That sounds good," I encouraged.

"My list is going to have just one thing on it. When that is accomplished, I'll move to step number two. I'll wait for the Lord to tell me step two. I can only do one step at a time, and I know what step one is!"

"Lord, let her tell me what it is," I prayed, feeling completely in the dark.

"Actually, I owe Sammy an apology."

I nearly fell out of my chair. Thelma apologize?

"But Sammy won't understand that. He might think I'm making fun of him, so I'll start with the one thing he'll understand. I can't do it, of course, but the Lord will do it for me." Thelma smiled the biggest smile I'd ever seen and explained, "I only have one thing to do. I will receive my husband."

I almost got up and danced on the table because I knew the instruction was straight from the Lord, who hadn't left us alone for a moment. Thelma smiled some more, and her body language relaxed. She laughed a little to herself. New joy filled her heart, and it showed plainly on her face. She said, "Receive," again to herself, or perhaps to the Lord.

The Holy Spirit nudged me. I would never have thought of this, but it was exactly what a logical person would need. I got up and removed from my bulletin board a small card. It said, "Oh, God, I cannot. You never said I could. Oh, God, You can. You always said You would." Turning it over, I said, "Let's write down the date and hour. Satan will attack you tomorrow and for a lot of tomorrows about this being real. We'll write it down." I wrote the date and hour. Eleven thirty! The whole thing had only taken an hour. Then

I printed in bold letters: "R E C E I V E." I opened my Bible to
Matthew 18:19 and said, "It works, Thelma. It has to. God says it
will. His Word is powerful." We laid our hands on the Word and I
prayed. I don't know exactly what I prayed, but it sealed what
Thelma had done, and the praying was so simple and easy that I
didn't want to stop. In fact, I didn't stop when the Holy Spirit said
to stop, and instantly I knew I was praying on my own and quickly
ended the prayer.

The next morning Thelma told me that she slept all night for the
first time in months. She looked rested and at peace. Three days
later she and her son left us.

I don't understand how a woman can come to the point of realizing she needs to apologize to an abusive, alcoholic husband. I don't
understand how she will receive him, as he is, but I believe with all
my heart that she will because Thelma learned that she mustn't attempt anything alone. Somehow I believe Thelma will see Sammy
with new eyes and she'll see him through the blood of Jesus. That
way, she'll see what he's *going to be*, not what he is. Step one will
be impossible unless Thelma leans heavily on Jesus.

# 21

## MORE RECEIVING

I thought a lot about Thelma and her determination to receive her husband with the Lord's help. The more I thought about it the more it seemed that I had overlooked something. The Holy Spirit kept bringing the episode to my mind. "Lord, I understand about receiving. I really do. I didn't when I was first married. We'd been married seventeen years before I understood receiving, but finally I did understand it."

But it was as though the Lord was telling me that there'd be something new I'd need to receive. I chalked the whole idea up to my emotional nature and tried to forget about receiving. Still, that word seemed to lodge in my mind.

The next day Jerry told me that he was considering coaching little-league football—the team our boys were on. If he'd told me he was considering raising rattlesnakes in the back yard, my reaction would have been about the same. I stared at him grimly, while all kinds of thoughts exploded in my mind. "You don't have time. We hardly see each other as it is. I've come so far with football—finally beginning to understand it a little, and I'm enthusiastic about the boys playing. I even go to practice. I don't take the tubes out of the television anymore when the big game comes on. How can you coach? You don't get home from work in time. The whole thing sounds impossible. Surely, you won't do this. I've given up so many of my rights. Let Jerry give up something. Let him give up this football coach idea."

I'd often looked at wives of football coaches and thought with relief, well, at least my husband isn't a football coach! It had taken me twenty years to accept football. I wasn't ready to accept Jerry as a coach.

He looked at me questioningly. I knew he'd probably do it with or without my blessing, but that he really wanted my support. In my mind I pictured the typical little-league coach's wife. She was at each practice and game with lots of Gatorade. She made clever comments about new plays and always had some word of encouragement for each boy. She knew them all by name, and they adored her. She screamed wildly at games.

I couldn't honestly give Jerry my support. I just couldn't. Later we talked about it a little. He sounded like he wasn't going to do it, and I smiled openly, telling him that that certainly sounded like a wise decision to me.

I woke up early the next morning. Jerry's usually up when I get up. But this morning he was just staring at the ceiling with his arms folded under his head. I didn't have to ask him what he was thinking about. I knew.

If only Thelma hadn't said she was going to receive Sammy and hadn't gotten so excited over the receiving principle, I could have come up with a dozen reasons why Jerry shouldn't coach.

We didn't talk about it anymore. Right up to the deadline of letting them put down his name as a coach, he didn't tell me what he was going to do. I could tell he was deep in prayer and thought, but we didn't pray together. I didn't even pray for him alone. My prayer would have been, "Lord, stop him, please." So I just didn't pray.

Jerry made a decision. He accepted the coaching offer.

One night at prayer meeting in our church we split into small groups, and I found myself praying about my attitude toward Jerry's coaching. Others prayed with me and while we sat there I began to see his coaching as a ministry. I asked the Lord to help us take Jesus onto the field. Finally at home that night, I asked the Lord to help me receive Jerry as a coach. I asked for enthusiasm. After my prayer I looked into the mirror and said, "Well, you still don't look like a coach's wife." But I bought an orange shirt (team color) and by the time I got the large orange Gatorade cooler full and a stack of paper cups under one arm, and grabbed the roster and started out to practice each day, I decided that no one could possibly know what a victory the Lord was giving me. One day I even appeared with two footballs, one helmet, and the kicking tee.

Our supper often had to be as late as nine. I had to be sure the boys were ready for practice at six fifteen, three days a week. I also had to have Jerry's clothes laid out, as he had about thirty seconds to change. Then we'd pile in the car and take off.

After two weeks of this, I was a little tired but, nevertheless, excited. One morning it was raining when I woke up, and the first thing I prayed for was that the rain would stop before time for practice. I was actually looking forward to it!

I got to know the mothers and players, some of the daddies too. When I typed up our roster, at the bottom I typed "they shall run, and not be weary . . ." (Isaiah 40:31, KJV). The cheerleaders made up a cheer about running and not being weary. The other coach's wife and I would pray daily for the team. It was fun taking the Lord into the area of football.

I was doing really well as a coach's wife, I thought. Then one evening after practice Jerry turned on the Monday night football game. We'd been at the field four nights in a row. I'd started going to the high school games each Friday night—even went an hour early so we'd get a good seat. Each Saturday our team played. Football equipment was in every closet. Many phone calls come to coaches and their wives relay the messages, I learned. And I did fine, until the Monday night game. All the children were in bed. I sat down and stared at Jerry. I'd hardly seen him in four or five weeks. He wasn't even aware that I had come into the den.

I felt the anger rising in me. I got up and silently left the room. I knew what to expect. I'd faced it before.

Self-pity.

It's always of Satan, and he knows just when to use it. Oh, how I wanted to feel sorry for myself. I deserved some attention from my husband. He hadn't said one word of praise, and I'd done a good job of being a coach's wife. By an act of my will I said, "I will not indulge in self-pity. I will praise the Lord in all situations." And I began to praise Him and thank Him that Jerry was coaching football. I longed to feel sorry for myself for just a few minutes, but I knew that it would be like quicksand. I'd been in its grip too many times before. I went to sleep praising and thanking God and thinking good thoughts about Jerry.

The next morning while I was cooking breakfast Jerry came in and put his arms around me from behind. It was such an unlikely thing for him to do with our morning schedule that I almost jumped. It was time for his car pool. He hugged me for a long time and said softly, "I love you and I appreciate you. Thank you for helping me and for being such a good football wife. You've done a great job of organizing things for me. Don't know what I'd do without you." Then he gave me a kiss and was gone.

After the door slammed I told myself it wasn't a dream or a daydream; it was real. Looking out the kitchen window I thought, "Wow, Lord, I can go all season on that. If Jerry doesn't say anything else to me, I have those words memorized." And somehow I realized that if I'd gone to sleep angry with him or feeling sorry for myself that I would never have heard those words. I decided to go ahead and mix the Gatorade for practice that night. Stirring it slowly I saw so clearly that the Lord was doing a miraculous work in me through being willing to become a football coach's wife. It all hinged on that word that Thelma had become so excited about: RECEIVE!

# 22

# FOR SOMEONE WHO NEEDS IT

"Oh, no," I gasped in horror as my daughter and I walked through the shopping center.

"What's the matter, Mother?" she asked.

"I've lost it. My pin that I love so much." I touched the place on my blouse where it had been. Just a few moments ago I'd glanced down at it.

"Oh, Mother," Julie groaned, knowing how much this pin meant to me.

A few months ago I'd seen an ad about the pin in the paper, torn it out and placed it on my bulletin board in the kitchen, hoping my husband would question me about it. When he didn't, I hinted openly. "I want that pin more than anything I've wanted in a long time."

"Well, get it," he said without looking at the ad.

"It's sort of expensive. The bank book doesn't look too good."

Jerry read the ad for the small pin that said simply **TRY GOD**. All proceeds from the sale went to rehabilitate delinquent girls in a home in New York. The home had a ninety-percent success record of leading girls into a personal relationship with God.

"Get it," Jerry smiled. "I want you to have it."

I sent my order off that day and awaited the arrival of the pin as eagerly as a child waiting for a prize from a cereal company. It came a week later from the exclusive jeweler's nestled in soft cotton and tissue paper. I put it on immediately.

Sometimes people asked about the pin and I got an opportunity to tell them what God was doing in my life. Many people glanced at it, then looked away quickly. But even if a word wasn't spoken, the little pin radiated a continuous silent message of love.

Now it was gone!

Julie and I ran around frantically in the huge department store trying to retrace our steps, even crawling under counters. I muttered to myself as I fought back tears. Finally, I turned in my name and a description at the Lost and Found. "It's really gone. I can't believe it."

Julie piped up, "Have you said, 'Thank You, Lord,' yet?"

Thanking God for all experiences, both good and bad, was a new principle our family was learning (1 Thessalonians 5:18). We've had some exciting times through praising God for *all* things. The more difficult the situation, the more fantastic the outcome. Usually I'm the one who fervently reminds my family to "Thank God, anyway." This time, however, I couldn't get beyond the pain. And Julie saw me hurting instead of trusting God and thanking Him.

Even as we left the shopping center my eyes darted over the floor of the mall, hoping I still might find the pin. *It's possible, Lord. You could show it to me even now.* I couldn't believe that God wasn't going to let me find my pin. In the car I looked through my clothing and purse, then on the floorboard.

Julie asked again, "Have you said, 'Thank You, Lord,' yet?"

I sighed, wishing that she weren't with me. But I answered honestly, "No."

"Well, can you thank Him for letting someone find that pin who really needs it? You know, maybe a person at a crucial point in his life, who needs a bit of encouragement. A sign, to know God is really working out an answer to some problem."

I had to smile at her. Nearly sixteen, she was now offering me some of the spiritual advice I'd been shoving at her lately.

"Can you do that, Mother?" she persisted. "Someone needs that pin, and that someone will be special, and the timing will be perfect in his life. Don't you believe God will do that?"

I wanted to, but remained so aware of my pain that I mumbled without enthusiasm, "Guess so." We drove home in silence. Every mile my mind seemed to shout, "your pin's gone . . . your pin's gone."

Three days later, while vacuuming, I prayed, "Lord, I'm making myself miserable about that pin. Now with Your help, I'm giving it up. Please do what Julie said. Let a person who is doubting You find it, and let that experience speak to that person in an exciting way." I smiled, thinking about someone reaching down and picking up such a tiny pin that could easily be overlooked. "Everything I have belongs to You, Lord, and now I give up this pin. Please give it to someone who really needs it." I began to feel a tinge of excitement as I mentally let go of my pin and trusted God to work some good out of my losing it. I forgot about the pin, but remembered to pray for the person who would find it. I didn't want that person to miss God's message, so I prayed for this unknown person often. My only regret became that I wouldn't know who found the pin. How I'd love to see this stranger finding it.

The next day I took Julie for a scheduled doctor's appointment. As we sat in the waiting room I read and swung one foot back and forth. I became aware of something under my foot and looked down, thinking the sole of my shoe was loose. I'd just bought the shoes a week ago and wondered if they were already tearing up.

Glancing down at the carpet, I blinked my eyes several times. My heart beat rapidly. I gasped loud and long. People stared at me.

I bent over and picked up my **TRY GOD** pin! In those few seconds a lot of thoughts crowded into my puzzled mind: "It's not my pin. I've found another one. How could it be mine? I don't know how. This is fantastic. Thank You, Lord."

And then the most powerful thought of all: *It's me! I'm the someone special who needed to find the pin.* As I held the pin lovingly in my hand, I didn't mind at all that it was scratched and worn-looking now.

As Julie and I marveled over finding the pin, we figured out what had happened. I'd been wearing the same soft-sole shoes the day I lost the pin as I had on today. The pin had stuck in the bottom of my shoe and I'd been walking around on it all this time! But only when I was willing to give it up, did I get it back.

I've tried God in many difficult situations more serious than losing a pin since that incident. He's always come through with flying colors.

# 23

## TAKE AS DIRECTED

As I undressed for bed I stared down at strange-looking welts across my chest. There were two patches on the front of me and, turning around and looking in the mirror, I saw one patch on my back. They were slightly sore to touch, and I remembered that several times during the day I'd felt deep pains that seemed to be underneath the welts. I had no idea what the eruptions were but, remembering that the children had recently gone through a stubborn case of impetigo, I quickly diagnosed my rash. I suspected it would need medication.

I phoned the doctor's office the next day and explained the problem to a nurse, hoping my doctor would prescribe medication without my having to go in. However, the nurse thought I should come in, so I made an appointment.

In the examining room the nurse looked at the welts with sudden seriousness and said, "I don't think that's impetigo. He'll be *right* in." The tone of her voice alarmed me. As I waited for the doctor, Satan took advantage of the situation. He fed thoughts into my already racing mind. *Not impetigo. Something more serious. You know how often you have to have mammograms. This could be advanced cancer. Gone all the way to the back.* I vividly remembered helping a woman dress who had advanced cancer, and I saw that the cancer had broken through the skin and oozed. My mouth suddenly became dry. Was I facing surgery? Death?

My doctor came in, made polite conversation, and then looked carefully at the skin disorder. *Lord, help me be brave.* The nurse watched silently, grimly, I thought. "This is not impetigo," he said flatly.

I tried to prepare myself for the words I expected to hear. I hoped he couldn't hear my heart beating.

He looked at me silently for a moment, then said, "You have shingles."

What was he saying? Shingles? Not cancer? What in the world were shingles? I'd heard of them, years ago. I had shingles. Whatever they were, I welcomed them. Praise the Lord for shingles. "Lord, how I praise You for shingles! Oh, happy day. I've got shingles," I thought.

I sat looking at the doctor and grinning silently. I thought for a moment that I was going to laugh out loud. The doctor must have picked up my giddy attitude. He said sternly, "This is serious. You are going to be in pain—a lot of pain. This is just the beginning. It's not bad now. Many people have to go in the hospital with shingles. I've seen two-hundred-pound men cry like babies. They are terribly painful."

I wiped the smile off my face, and my mind raced ahead of him. "Well, give me a prescription. We've caught this case of shingles in time. Write me out a prescription and let me get out of here."

"Unfortunately," he continued, looking even more stern now, "there is no medication for shingles. Nothing I can give you. Just pain medicine. You'll want to stay in bed as the pain gets worse. What are you allergic to?"

"No medication," I thought wildly. "He's not going to write me out a prescription." I could see the prescription in my mind. "Take four times a day as needed for pain." Almost every pain medicine made me terribly sleepy. I couldn't imagine three weeks of that.

"Are you allergic to anything?" he repeated the question.

How foolish it suddenly seemed to go home and wait for expected pain. It was like sitting on a railroad track waiting to be hit by the train. Why not move off the track? In a split second I decided and *knew* (not hoped) that I simply would not need any medication. A scripture came to my mind: ". . . by whose stripes ye were healed" (1 Peter 2:24, KJV). *Were*, not will be. I'd just recently discovered that scripture. Sitting on the examining table looking right at the doctor, I knew positively there was no need for me to take pain medicine. I also knew that the shingles that were now on me would soon disappear and that there would be no more. I'd never been so sure of anything. I didn't understand it. Nothing like this had happened to me before. I knew also that if my doctor had written out a prescription that would cure the shingles, I would have taken it without question.

But there was no medicine available so I would simply rely on
God's medicine. I'd never done that before. The idea didn't seem to
be completely mine. I was healed. I wanted to laugh. It was so
simple. I hadn't prayed fervently, or strained to understand. I
hadn't done anything, it seemed.

The doctor was waiting for me to say something. "I don't want
that pain medicine. I'm not going to need it."

"I'm almost certain that you will. Well, you can phone the office
and I'll call you in something when the pain starts."

"I'm not going to be sick or in pain. These shingles are going
away. No more are coming." I couldn't believe I said that to a doctor. But I knew I was right.

He smiled a little. "Well, what's that? The power of positive
thinking?"

"Positive prayer." I smiled. "You'll see." Even though I knew I
was well, I planned to call a few friends to agree with me in prayer.
I knew Satan would attack again.

The doctor seemed exasperated with me. "If you aren't the
sickest you've ever been, phone and let me know. You'll be one of
the first to have shingles like this and not need pain medication."

I nodded and still felt like laughing. His words didn't apply to
me anymore. There would be no pain. It was settled.

My husband was astonished that I'd refused anything for pain.
He asked over and over, "Do they hurt yet?"

"Nope," was always my answer. I'm not brave. I have a very low
pain level. For several days Jerry would look at the splotches. One
day he said, "They're going away!"

"Yep," I agreed. I kept marveling over how I hadn't done anything. The healing wasn't even a big deal. It was such a simple,
quick thing. Usually I've struggled over any kind of prayers of
healing and prayed them cautiously. "Exactly how does healing
work?" I'd wondered. "Is it for everyone?" I remembered that I was
very relaxed and joyful on the inside because I didn't have cancer. I
was praising the Lord quietly in my heart for the shingles. After I
got home, I did call two friends who believed in healing and they
prayed with me on the phone. One of them laughed, "You're
healed, Marion. I know you are."

In less than a week the skin eruptions were completely gone and

I'd felt no pain. I even stopped looking at the fading patches when I dressed. Jerry asked one day, "Three weeks up yet?"

"Not quite," I'd answered. When the three weeks were up Jerry said, "I think you should call the doctor and tell him about this . . . healing."

My Jerry saying that. That wasn't his kind of language or belief. He was always after me for making things too simple and believing almost anything. So when *he* said to call the doctor and confirm the healing, I knew I was supposed to.

I was a little apprehensive about calling. To tell friends who understood and believed like I did was one thing. But to call a doctor's office and tell someone over the phone—well, that was something else. Nevertheless, I dialed the familiar number and when the nurse answered, she sounded very busy and efficient. I said, "Hi, this is Marion West. I was there three weeks ago with shingles."

"Do you need something for pain?" she asked.

"No, actually I'm all well. Well, I wasn't really sick. I was healed."

Dead silence.

I continued, "The Lord healed me, and the doctor said he wanted me to call him back and let him know how I was in three weeks. All the shingles went away a week after I saw him and no more came, and I didn't have any pain, or take any medicine, and I just wanted to call and tell the doctor."

Silence.

"Well, I've never been healed before. I think it's pretty exciting."

"Oh, me too. I think it's great," she said with enthusiasm. "I'll tell the doctor right away. Let me see if I have it straight." She went over what I'd said. She didn't sound so busy now.

"That's right. Thank you. Bye."

That experience was like a tiny bit of new light that I'd never walked in before. It was so incredibly simple—almost funny, too. I just didn't do anything but remember that scripture, but I held on to it like a determined little bulldog. I wish I could explain it adequately. I can't. I just know that when I learned no medicine was available I leaned totally on the Lord and His Word.

# 24

## HOGWASH

My mother planned a visit with us and I'd been thinking about taking her to a church across town to visit. Jerry wasn't so sure I should, but I couldn't seem to get rid of the idea. Julie encouraged me to take her. I'd only been a few times. I didn't know how to explain the services to my mother. That's when the idea of taking her to the church plopped right down into my mind.

I hadn't definitely made up my mind what to do when Sunday arrived. We attended our church on Sunday morning. By Sunday afternoon I had asked the Lord to work out the details if He wanted me to take Mother to the church across town. Jerry and the children didn't want to go. I couldn't find it by myself. Our chances of going looked slim.

The church was of another denomination than ours, but the people who attended and belonged came from many denominations as well as from none. I'd never heard denomination mentioned. The first time I'd gone with friends I'd been a little self-conscious. Everyone seemed more enthused than I. It seemed people were watching me, but of course they weren't.

About four thirty a friend—I'll call her Helen—phoned and said right away that she was going to this church that night. I about dropped the telephone because Helen had believed and taught in no uncertain terms against some of the practices of this church. She'd been cool toward me when she knew I had visited. The joy in her voice was unmistakable, "The Lord is setting me free from bondage, Marion. Bill [her husband] too. We've been through hell. Bill can't go tonight. He's out of town, but I'm going with the children, another couple and their three children. Will you go?"

That's when I explained about my mother visiting.

"Bring her," Helen insisted. "She'll love it."

"She's never been to anything like . . . that, Helen."

"Bring her."

"Let me talk to her and I'll call you right back."

"I'll pray," she said and hung up.

Mother agreed to go immediately, and Jerry looked at me gravely. We hurried to get dressed. "We have to get there an hour early to get a seat," I explained to my mother.

"Why, I've never heard of such a thing. We have so few on Sunday night."

Helen and her friends and their six children picked us up a few minutes before six. I hadn't explained anymore about the church to Mother. When we parked, Mother asked, "Why is everyone hurrying? What's the traffic jam about?"

"They're hurrying to get a seat, Mother, and there's always a traffic jam at this church." A policeman helped us park and we hurried along with the crowd. There were "No parking on the grass" signs. Mother stopped for a moment and exclaimed, "Oh, the church is beautiful. I was expecting—something else." Inside we found seats and Mother kept marveling that the church was filling up on a Sunday night. It held over two thousand. We watched people greeting one another for an hour. Then the service began.

On the first hymn, one woman near us held up her hand. I saw her, and I saw my mother watching her. Hers was the only hand up right then. My mother leaned over and asked me, "What's she doing?"

"Now, Lord," I thought, "what am I going to say?"

"It's a good question. Answer it," the Lord seemed to say to me.

"She's worshiping the Lord," I whispered.

"Oh," Mother said.

In a little while more hands went up. Suddenly the pastor began singing "Learning to Lean" and the congregation joined in. The song wasn't announced and it wasn't on the program.

When I'd visited this church before, they'd sung that song and it always touched me in a powerful way. For one thing, I was trying to make up my mind to write this book. I'd played the song on the stereo for my mother, and she knew I was considering doing a book with that title.

Suddenly she turned to me, and her face crumpled and she

smiled at the same time. It was a unique expression that I'd seldom seen on her. Joy and anguish mixed. "Mannie," she whispered, "you and I better hold our hands up."

I couldn't believe it. My mother! Apparently without any struggle or reservation either. "Go ahead, Mother," I urged.

"You do it with me," she asked.

I'd raised my hand before. I could do it or not do it, but most of the times my arm got tired and I felt I owed people an explanation. I don't have to raise my hand to worship.

My mother and I raised our right hands—high. This time was unlike any other time I'd ever raised my hand in worship and praise. It was set apart. The moment I lifted my hand, I wanted to touch the ceiling. I had to keep my hand lifted. I couldn't put it down this time. My arm never tired. "Oh, Lord," I prayed, "let them sing all night." I never wanted to take my hand down. We sang and sang, and God's love surrounded us snugly.

Without warning, Helen grabbed me. She was crying. I'd never seen her cry. She was a fantastic Bible teacher and one of the most knowledgeable people I'd ever known. A friend of ours said, "If you had diarrhea, Helen would have a scripture for the occasion." She could quote scripture all day and night. She had every translation of the Bible in print. I admired her a lot.

Now Helen's mascara was running and she made noises crying. She grabbed me and sobbed, "Oh, Marion, thank you for loving me just like I am. I've been such a spiritual snob—so wrong. God is breaking me. It hurts, but I'm going to be whole at last—finally. He's got something more for me—and for Bill."

I hugged her back with one arm. I wasn't about to take my other hand down. Then I wiped away a few tears, and we all continued singing.

The service lasted two hours. No one in the entire sanctuary seemed in any hurry to go home. We applauded some of the things the minister said. So many people responded to the altar call that they asked people to stand, not kneel, to make room for more people. The sermon had been about depression and how God could heal it.

We all piled back into the car. A policeman helped us get out into the highway and we started home. It was an hour's drive. We were talking, laughing—even singing.

"Well," Helen said, "I guess I've blown it at our church. They will find out I've been over here, and we won't be welcomed back. They won't understand. I know how they feel . . . I didn't understand for so long. I've been wrong."

My mother turned to her and said, "What in the world are you talking about? Just go back and tell them about this beautiful service. I can't ever remember having such a wonderful time in church. It was different, but—real. It *was* real, Helen."

Helen smiled. "I know, but they don't understand, and we won't be welcomed back in our church. This will finish us off."

My mother looked at Helen intently, then said matter of factly, "Hogwash! This country was founded on religious freedom!"

"What?" Helen laughed.

"Hogwash," my mother repeated the word with more force. "I'm going back and tell the people at my church about this other church that I visited. I'm so glad I came. I'm going to tell lots of people."

Helen hugged my mother and exclaimed, "Hogwash, Mrs. Grogan. Isn't God wonderful! Praise the Lord!"

And a few weeks later when Doubleday wanted me to do this book, I called my mother and said, "Mother, Doubleday wants me to write *Learning to Lean* for them. I don't know what to say. The book's not written. I'm not sure I can do it—"

She interrupted with exploding joy in her voice, "Hogwash! Of course you can do it. Have you forgotten the night in that church when we raised our hands and sang 'Learning to Lean'? That song was for *you*. Tell them you'll do the book!"

# 25

## OBEDIENCE

For over a year I'd been attending a nondenominational luncheon once a month. The food was good, and the Christian fellowship was super. The first time I'd met Cora Cummings, when she prayed for me in the shopping mall, she'd asked me if I'd speak at a Christian Fellowship luncheon. The old fear of speaking tried to rise up in me, but I'd been saying "yes" a lot lately when asked to give my testimony. And I was so grateful to Cora, so I told her that I would.

She greeted me warmly at the luncheon as did other strangers. We sang and prayed and sang some more. I was sitting at the head table with Cora, but I'd been having such a good time that I forgot I was the speaker. I just plain forgot, until Cora stood to introduce me. That had never happened before. I told the group that I'd forgotten to be nervous, and they laughed and clapped. Someone said, "Thank You, Jesus."

I'd continued going to the luncheons. I love to hear testimony and each month they had someone to give their testimony.

On this particular meeting I attended with a heavy heart but a bright smile. I wanted to appear to be a happy, radiant Christian. After all, I'd given my testimony, and I didn't want people to see me down. Something was bothering me deep within my soul, and I couldn't pray it away. An incident had happened a few weeks previous. I had offended someone, and the person let me know right away in an anger-filled voice. I knew immediately that I must apologize, even if I hadn't been wrong or meant to offend. And I was truly sorry about the whole thing. I would do anything to make things right between us again. And if I didn't apologize on the spot, I'd just have to return and do it later. God had been dealing with me about apologies.

This was the first person who'd refused to accept my apology. The anger remained. It hung in the air. Nothing I said helped.

I'd wake up in the middle of the night reliving the scene. Could I have said or done something else to make things right? "Yes," Satan would urge. "You didn't do enough." I'd think about it during the day, and when I read my Bible. Thoughts like, "You've separated yourself from God; He can't hear your prayers now; you can't speak anymore or write or teach Sunday school; you've really boo-booed; everything you do now will be in the flesh, and without the Spirit's help." Finally Satan spat out at me, "God doesn't love you. Maybe He never did. You don't belong to Him anymore. You're alone."

"No, no, no," I would cry out in my heart and read my Bible. "Nothing can separate me from His love. He loves me with an everlasting love." I'd be okay for a while, but the attacks came again and again, and I sank lower and lower until I felt uncomfortable with Christians. Yet, I couldn't seem to explain my dilemma. Several Christian friends had said simply, "Forget about it. You apologized. You know how Satan likes to make you feel guilty. You should know better than this."

But instead of helping, I felt even worse, because I did know better.

The guests at the luncheon were six black women from an Atlanta church. They gave testimony and sang. Their songs were so anointed and powerful that I cried without even expecting to. The testimonies were so honest that they were painful to hear. All pride had been stripped from the people speaking. Their honesty was astounding. They sang and praised the Lord in a way I'd never seen, as though we weren't even there and they stood in the very presence of God.

The strange thing was that from the moment they entered the room, one of the women really caught my eye. I don't know why. I just stared at her. Maybe because her face was so love-filled. I suddenly hoped that when she walked by my table with her tray of food that she would smile at me. "Lord, let her smile at me." She walked by and smiled—at someone else! I felt crushed. Why couldn't I reach out and grab her hand and simply speak to her? Then, when I saw her sit down at the piano, I was even more in awe of her. I'm so unmusical. People that have musical ability usually make me feel inadequate. Oh, she played with such unreserved joy. I began to have a sudden impulse to hug her. At the meeting,

they usually told us to go hug someone. I decided I'd hug the
woman at the piano when they told us to hug someone. But they
never told us to. "Go hug her anyway," a gentle voice urged.

"No. I can't. She won't understand. I wish I knew something to
say."

"Just hug her," came the suggestion once again.

"No."

However, all during the meeting I kept wishing I could hug this
woman. It was about time to go home, and I gathered up my Bible
and purse to leave. I'd decided not to get in the prayer line. "I'll be
all right," I told myself. But deep inside, I knew everything wasn't
all right at all. Suddenly the woman at the piano got up and came
over to me. She put her hand on my arm and asked in a soft voice,
"Sister, are you leaving?"

"Yes," I answered.

I noticed her eyes were filled with tears. "Then I must obey the
Spirit." She bowed her head—I did too—and she prayed, "Father,
in the name of Jesus, I ask You to let Your child become aware of
Your love for her in a new, fresh way. Satan, in the name of Jesus, I
command you to leave her alone. Take your hands off her. She is
His property. She doesn't have to live under guilt and fear. She's
been set free."

We opened our eyes and she explained, "I had to do it. The Spirit
told me to. I had to obey."

"Then I must obey too," I said joyfully. "He's told me to hug you
since you first came into the room." I hugged her, and she hugged
me back and said quietly, "Praise God." When we let go, she said,
"The Lord always sends one person just to hug me wherever I
minister. I waited. No one came today."

"I'm sorry," I said. "I just couldn't move. I've been—"

She stopped me. "It's all right now. You are fine now. Your guilt
and fear are gone, honey. You still belong to Him. Always will."

I nodded happily, and she hugged me again.

I don't even know her name. I just know that she listens to the
voice of God and obeys. She led me out of despair and gloom that
had me trapped.

We almost missed each other. I was too wrapped up in myself to
obey and hug her, but, praise God, she'd learned to obey.

# 26

## DO YOU UNDERSTAND THE ROSE?

Finishing up in the kitchen after supper, I looked forward to relaxing for a few minutes. Just as I was about to turn off the light, the phone rang. I answered and heard, "Mrs. West, it's Jenny." Her voice was filled with fear.

What in the world could be the matter? All sorts of things crossed my mind. I didn't know Jenny very well. I was her Sunday school teacher—her new teacher. She didn't know me well, either. Jenny hadn't missed a single Sunday. I always had her undivided attention when I taught. All the girls listened politely—almost too politely. They just sat there staring at me without saying a word. I didn't know if I was getting through to them or not.

"Jenny, what's wrong? Can I help you?" I asked over the phone.

"Mrs. West, I'm soooo scared. I'm at the school and—"

"Oh, Jenny," I interrupted, "you're in the Miss Freshman Parkview Pageant, aren't you?"

"Yes, ma'am. And I wish I'd never entered. I'm shaking all over. I can't even walk." Her voice quivered tearfully.

Still stunned that she'd called me, I said, "Oh, I wish I'd known you were going to be in the contest. I would have come to see you."

"I'd give anything if you were here now. *Anything.*"

"Jenny, it starts in fifteen minutes, and I'm not even dressed. I have on jeans, no makeup. I can't possibly make it."

"That's okay. I shouldn't expect you to come. But could you just talk to me for a few minutes . . . like we are in Sunday school? I'm so scared I can't smile or walk."

"Is it very important to you to win?" I asked.

"Oh, no. I just want to be able to walk out there and smile."

"Can I pray with you?"

"Yes, ma'am."

Jenny was calling from a phone booth outside the school. In my mind I could see her standing in the booth dressed in a formal gown with her head bowed.

"Dear Lord, we know fear is not from You. You say in Your Word that You give us a spirit of love.* Give Jenny Your love right now, and, Jesus, we believe that You'll walk onto that stage with her. We're trusting You to smile through Jenny. In Jesus' name, amen."

"Thanks, Mrs. West. Gotta go. See you Sunday."

The line went dead. I looked at the clock. The pageant started in less than fifteen minutes. The school was four minutes away. Suddenly I wasn't tired anymore. I ran up the steps, flung my clothes off, and grabbed an outfit that's easy to get into. I always grab it when I have to hurry. I daubed on some makeup, patted my hair, and called out to Jerry, "I'm going to the pageant at the school."

Parking my car in the large lot, I ran all the way to the school gym. I hurried so that I went in the wrong door and found myself backstage. All the young contestants stood around helping each other get ready. I saw Jenny about the same time she saw me. She ran across the room and flung her arms around me. "You came!" With her arm still around me, she said, "Girls, this is my Sunday school teacher, Mrs. West."

The girls looked me over and didn't seem too impressed. I noticed that four other girls in my class were in the contest. I spoke to each of them. Then I whispered to Jenny, "I look terrible. I didn't have time to dress, but I just had to come."

"Oh, you look wonderful to me. I can't believe you're really here."

"You're going to be fine, Jenny. I just know you are. I'll sit out there and keep praying for you. Remember, Jesus will walk anywhere with you and you can lean on Him." Jenny was a cheerleader. I got a sudden inspiration. "Just like in the cheer, Jenny." I leaned way to one side and cheered quietly, "Lean, lean, lean, lean, lean, lean, lean! Lean, lean, lean, lean, lean!"

She nodded her head and squeezed my hand. "I'll lean, Mrs. West."

I sat in the audience, and when Jenny walked out on the stage I almost gasped out loud. On top of being calm, she was smiling one of the most radiant smiles I'd ever seen . . . like she knew a won-

* II Timothy 1:7.

derful secret. Her smile was real, natural. Sitting out in the darkened auditorium, I had to smile too, just looking at her.

When the winners were finally announced and they had stepped out from the lineup, Jenny's name hadn't been called. Nevertheless, that glowing smile continued as though her mind was on something else apart from the contest.

After the pageant, I hugged Jenny and told her how lovely she'd been. She just kept smiling like she'd won. "I wasn't afraid, Mrs. West! Really. Jesus walked with me. He took away my fear. I couldn't keep from smiling. You really can lean on Him." She hugged me and said, "I love you."

Sunday, Jenny was the first one at Sunday school. After the class started, I asked, as always, "Anyone want to share anything?"

So far no one had spoken. They just sat and stared at me. Jenny startled everyone by saying, "I do." She began telling about her fears before the pageant. The other girls who were in it nodded in agreement. As she explained what had happened and that she'd called me, she began crying, but she kept on telling the story in between sobs.

The class listened in awe. Even while Jenny cried, she smiled. "Jesus is real all right, and He'll go with you anywhere. I'd rather have had Him walking on that stage with me than to have won! I don't want to do anything without Him—ever."

Things haven't been quite the same in class since Jenny shared her experience. Other girls have begun to share their fears too. Sometimes a girl will speak out in class, looking almost fearful as she talks. Then the most amazed, happy look crosses her face when the other girls nod and agree with her. They're discovering that everyone has fears but that Jesus can get them through anything. They've been honest beyond belief.

On the last Sunday I taught that class before they were promoted, Jenny came into class and laid a red rose in my lap. "I can't say all the words. Do you understand this rose?"

I nodded and held onto it the whole class hour. Then I took it to church and held it some more. Looking at the rose I knew full well what it meant. At the age of fourteen, Jenny was learning to lean.

# 27

# THE "WRITE" WAY

I'm convinced that my twin sons fought before they were born. I was never able to make the doctor believe me, but he was aware of the fact that I experienced a cracked rib before they were born.

Julie and Jennifer had been easy children to discipline. They minded me, played together for hours, and seldom argued. I had little patience with mothers whose children fought. I'd always think to myself, "If those were my children, I'd certainly straighten them out. No excuse for children fighting."

I had liked the nice comments people made about how well behaved our little girls were, and I thought I was a super mom. Then when the girls were five and seven, the twins were born.

When we got them home from the hospital, we put Jon and Jeremy in the same crib. They'd been so close for so long, we decided to separate them gradually. There wasn't the slightest chance of ever getting them mixed up. They didn't even look like cousins. During the first few weeks at home, they would manage to work their way to the center of the baby bed, even though I'd placed them far apart. It was as though they argued when only a few weeks old. They would kick, scratch, and poke one another. By the time they were six weeks old, we had to put them in separate cribs.

They started walking at nine months, holding on to furniture. As they explored and played, inevitably one wanted what the other one had. If one twin stood in a certain spot in the room, the other twin wanted to stand right there and would push his brother out of the way. One day when they were a few months older, Jon slammed Jeremy's finger in a closet door and it required five stitches to close the cut. Another time, Jon wouldn't give Jeremy a toy and Jeremy got so angry that he ran head on into a table and cut his head. He had four stitches and asked on the way to the hospital, "Can I have my toy back now?"

Once Jeremy became so frustrated and angry that he climbed onto the mantel in the den. As I ran for him, he leaped onto the brick fireplace. I knew he did it on purpose. When I picked him up, he asked, dazed, "Will you make Jon give me my duck back now?" Three stitches closed the wound in his head.

For a while I dressed them alike, but they fought over clothes anyway. One shirt would be softer than the other. They fought over what to have for breakfast and when to take naps. There was a favorite highchair (they looked identical to me) and they argued over who got the "best" one.

As the boys got older, I'd try to reason with them, spank them, send them to their rooms, and finally sometimes end up screaming at them. I guess I was really screaming at myself and my failure to be able to discipline them.

At the dinner table they would fight over who got to sit by their daddy. They did this in church, too. They started using words like "dummy" and "stupid." Once they fought over a jacket and tore it in half.

And yet, deep down I believed they loved each other. Jon threw a rock (he said accidentally) and hit Jeremy in the face. The blood came so fast that for a few minutes I couldn't locate the wound. While I tried to find it, I saw Jon out of the corner of my eye. My concern for him was almost as great as for Jeremy. Jon stood motionless and asked over and over, "Is he okay?" Jeremy was all right, even though he required a few stitches, and I saw the relief flood through Jon. When the boys played football and one of them didn't get up after a play, often the other one would run over and check on him, then tell me, "He's okay, Mama."

Still, on the way home from practice we might have to stop the car so I could settle an argument over a football helmet.

Often, I didn't know which one to punish. They'd both insist it was the other one's fault, so I'd punish both of them, and one was probably innocent. I didn't feel good about that. Once when the boys were in the tub together, Jon held Jeremy's head under the water and he got choked. When I ran into the bathroom, Jon said, "Well, he turned hot water on me."

"Did not."

"You put soap in my eye on purpose."

"It was an accident," Jeremy screamed.

"Lord, there's got to be some kind of answer," I prayed finally.

"They're ten years old and the fighting isn't getting better. I wonder if there might be something I haven't thought of—something to dissolve my anger and theirs. We're in a circle of anger."

Watching Jerry and the boys out in the yard one day, I began to see that I didn't take up enough time with them. All their interests seemed foreign to me. Ball, frogs, lizards, fishing, pocketknives, tree huts, gardens, camping out—things like that aren't my favorite things, so I just stayed in the background and let Jerry handle those areas. My areas seemed to consist of: "Did you brush your teeth, get your lunch money, put on a jacket, you can't wear those pants, take out the trash, eat your beans."

It looked like a hopeless situation to me. Cleaning out the attic one day I picked up one of Julie's first little ballet slippers and held it for a long time. "Why," I thought, "I've always enjoyed the things that my girls did—even when they were small." Dolls, pretty dresses, ballet, piano, tea parties, playhouses, color books were my kind of things. Even now, I love to hear Julie relate what it is like to work for a veterinarian. And Jennifer and I have long conversations about hair styles, makeup, and dating. Sadly, I realized that the boys and I just didn't have much in common, except that I was their mother. Maybe since they were little fellows they'd sensed that. Maybe they fought all the time to get my attention. That was hard to swallow, but I did it, sitting there in the attic holding the ballet slipper. I resolved that something would link us together. I came out of the attic and started supper. Looking out the kitchen window I saw Jon working hard in a small vegetable garden his father had helped him start. Jon had asked me several times to come look at his garden and somehow . . . I never had. Jeremy sat in the tree house that Jerry had helped him build. He held on to a rope about to swing out like Tarzan. My boys' ball gloves and ball were by the kitchen door. Sitting on my kitchen stool, I reached over and picked up the ball and tossed it gently around in my hand, as if some marvelous answer were going to be revealed to me.

I began to take stock of my world, my interests. Quickly I knew that my world often revolved around reading and writing. I read continually and am usually busy at the typewriter trying to get my ideas on paper. I love words, phrases, dictionaries, my thesaurus. I even love notebook paper. I like the way it feels and smells.

Jon and Jeremy don't enjoy reading like the girls did. And they think I'm "different" from other mothers because I write. I thought back to when they were very young. I must have always had a book in my hand, thinking it made no difference.

A couple of days later Jon and Jeremy got into an argument about whose turn it was to take out the garbage. I made Jon take it. When he got back, I had a new type of discipline to try on them. I hoped it would bring us closer. I didn't expect it would be easy. I told both the boys very calmly, "I want each of you to write a two-page essay about obeying me and why it's important."

*Zounds!* All my anger vanished. The boys looked at me for a few minutes. "Write," they bellowed, but even as they complained, they grew quieter as they searched for paper and pencils. For half an hour there was glorious silence. They only got a page done on that first assignment. Finally, they gave them to me and hung over my shoulder while I read their work. It felt good to have them standing so close to me. Part of Jon's read: "So if your mother tells you to take out the garbage, do it, even if there isn't any garbage or if it's not your turn."

A line from Jeremy's read: "Obeying your mother is important because mothers do a lot of nice things for you and the Bible says to obey your Mama and Daddy . . ."

Even though their handwriting and spelling weren't good, I told them joyfully, "You have good ideas, boys." Their faces brightened as I praised them. I had them make all the necessary corrections, looking up misspelled words.

On the way to the grocery store the next day, the boys started a fight about who got to sit by which window. They both look alike to me, but one is obviously the better window. I announced calmly: "When we get home, each of you write a page explaining some good qualities in your brother. More fussing will result in an additional page."

Each boy scrambled to opposite windows, sat erect, and looked straight ahead.

All summer I had the boys write essays. Their sentence structure improved. So did the content of what they wrote. Sometimes I let them choose the topics. I knew what to expect: football. A few times I asked them to write about some emotion. They had trouble with this at first. Seems like little boys are taught not to express such ideas. Gradually, though, they learned to write about love, gratitude, and forgiveness.

The first day the boys came home from school this year, they came running inside yelling, "Guess what? The teacher had us write a theme at school about our summer and I could do it!"

Just recently Jeremy decided to do a report. It wasn't assigned. He just selected a favorite topic, dinosaurs, and did a beautiful essay, complete with drawings.

I had a small fit over his project, and we talked about it for a long time. I'm learning about frogs, snakes, fertilizer, space, and baseball and football—all sorts of things that I used to think were dull.

Recently Jon wrote an essay (his own title): "Why I'm Glad I Have a Brother."

Having the boys write links us together and is a miracle-working form of discipline for my boys.

The following are samples of essays written by Jon and Jeremy. The first one was assigned in church when Jon continued to misbehave during communion. I asked him several times to be quiet. Finally I whispered, "When we get home, I want a two-page essay on the Cross." He quit talking, looked straight ahead, and as soon as we got home he wrote the following essay:

> Here is the story of the cross as I know it.
> Back a long, long time ago there lived a man called Jesus.
> He was the Savior of the world. He was sent by His Father to preach the word of the Lord. This man never sinned at all.
> He saved people's lives.
> The people said that Jesus did things bad, but He didn't.
> They took Him to a king named Pilot. When they brought Jesus to him, Pilot didn't know what to do. He couldn't find nothing wrong with the man. So he gave the Savior to the people because he wanted to please them.
> Before they crucified Him, they whipped Him. Then they made Him carry a big cross up a hill. When they got to the top of the hill they nailed Him to the cross.
> He died in three hours.
> Then after He was buried He arose in three days!

That same day we ate lunch out after church. Jeremy pointed to a midget and said, "Look." The woman didn't hear Jeremy, but I assigned him an essay on different kinds of people.

He wrote:

Not all people act the same way as you do. Some are deaf. Some are retarded. Some are blind. Some are handicapped.

And there are many other different kinds of people. And they do not like for people to point at them and talk about them. They want to be treated just like you.

You would not like to be treated bad. You would like to be treated just like any other person if you were handicapped. People want to be treated like God would treat His children with loving care. You can help handicapped people by praying for them. Many handicapped people will even ask you to pray for them. Some of them have to use all their strength just to pray for themselves. Many of them can't even bow their heads.

But they can do things in a different way like in the paper it showed a boy that was born armless and wrote with his feet and he was a straight A student.

So do not treat anyone meanly. Treat them like God would.

One morning Jon sat on my kitchen stool putting on his shoes, before school. I always sit there and drink a cup of coffee and "wake up." "Jon, let me sit there," I asked.

"I got it first," he replied.

I gave him a mini-lecture on manners and on giving his seat to women gladly and I assigned him a theme to write on manners.

After school, he wrote for a while and handed me this:

Manners is a very important word.

The word doesn't mean much if you don't do it.

When you have good manners people will like you better.

Having good manners is a way of getting along with people better.

When you show good manners it also looks nice. Here are some good manners:

Ladies first.

Talk nice.

Hold your fork and spoon right.
There are many more.

When Jeremy lost a new, expensive jacket that he'd had only one week, I sent him out to look for it. After he found it, he had to write an essay on losing things. A portion of his essay said:

If you lose a jacket you will just have to be cold that winter. And if you lose school work you will have to do it all over. If you do lose something and find it, you will not be in as much trouble. Losing things is one of the most biggest problems in the whole entire world . . .

# 28

# MISSION OF LOVE

Without enthusiasm I dressed for the evening church service. Then I sat grimly in our living room swinging one foot waiting for my husband. We'd had an argument, and I was furious with him. I'd needled him about a matter until he'd shouted out at me in anger.

I didn't want to go to church. I'd already decided not to speak to my husband. I wasn't even going to share my hymnal with him. *Nothing* could possibly change my attitude. Church would simply be a meaningless ritual. With my attitude worship was impossible.

We drove in silence to church, both staring straight ahead. We were greeted warmly by several people as we entered. My halfway weak smile required tremendous effort. I hoped no one else smiled at me. I couldn't respond. Jerry didn't seem too enthusiastic either. I walked rapidly ahead of my husband and found a seat. Someone stopped him and so I sat alone while he talked with a friend.

I turned around slightly as a family came in and sat behind me. When I did, Donna Brandenburg smiled right at me.

Donna! *Of all people.* I'd taught her in a Sunday school class a few years ago. Donna was genuine. She didn't fake anything. One Sunday morning she'd asked me, "What happened to your hair? It looks terrible."

Her honesty had amused me and I'd laughed. Then she laughed too, and added, "I like you anyway." Donna always spoke to me in church, and sometimes she'd give me an impromptu hug. She had the most amazing capacity to love I'd ever seen.

Donna is a Down's syndrome child.

She leaned over the pew and whispered, "I want to sit with you." She'd never sat with me before in church. Her mother started to protest but I begged, "Oh, please let her." I suddenly desperately needed Donna to sit with me, and I didn't understand why.

Her mother gave permission, and Donna came and sat close to me. Before she sat down, though, she leaned over and hugged me

long and hard. It felt wonderful. When I hugged her back I felt an
unmistakable spark of joy in my cold, angry heart.

Donna smiled at me, and with some effort I returned her smile.
She looked at me silently. The look said, *You can do better than
that.*

Jerry joined us, sitting on the other side of Donna. She leaned
over and whispered, "Who's he?"

"My husband," I answered. She looked him over from head to toe
and then offered him one of her fantastic smiles. Out of the corner
of my eye, I saw Jerry's face burst into a smile. It didn't fade completely as the minister began preaching.

Throughout the service I'd feel Donna looking at me. Each time I
glanced down at her, she'd smile—totally, completely, without reservation. I could almost feel her loving me. She'd smile at Jerry,
too.

It got harder and harder not to return her unreserved smiles. Finally, it became easier to smile back at her and really mean it.
Donna didn't give up easily. We must have smiled at least twenty
times!

While we were singing, I felt the last bit of resistance and anger
collapse from around my heart.

It was an exquisite moment. An unexpected tear plopped right
onto the songbook that Donna and I were singing from. She looked
up at me quickly with concern. I wiped the other tears away and
gave Donna my biggest smile. It came straight from my heart.

She nodded her head in delight and smiled once more. That
beautiful, determined child just never seemed to tire of smiling.

No one in church, except Donna, could have gotten a smile out of
me. I'd fully intended to hold on to my anger. But Donna's love-
filled smiles were just too much. The anger had to vacate my heart,
and it felt wonderful to have it filled with love once again.

When church was over, I looked down and Donna had slipped
back to her mother. The place where Donna had been sitting was
still warm. Without a word she'd transformed two tight-lipped,
angry people into a smiling couple who left church holding hands.

Driving home from church, still holding hands, I wondered if the
Lord doesn't often send Donna on some of His more difficult mis-
sions of love.

# 29

# SOMETHING IN LIFE
# I HAVEN'T FOUND YET

Suddenly I wanted to run back out into the cold rain. The inside of the prison was overwhelmingly drab and dirty. My noble idea of "adopting" a young man at a nearby prison seemed foolish now and I wondered, what are we doing here? A heaviness hung in the air. Only a handful of relatives had come to visit inmates. Young men dressed alike huddled close to their families.

Chaplain Grant had explained that we were now considered Tommy's family.* He added that some prisoners received no visitors or mail—ever.

A few months ago I'd heard the chaplain speak when he visited our city. The idea of becoming acquainted with a young man from his prison planted itself stubbornly in my mind. My family had shown mild interest when I explained to them what I wanted to do. Jerry gave me a go-ahead to contact the chaplain with my idea.

He said that our request was most unusual but that we could have an inmate assigned to us. "I've already begun to look for him. In the meantime, write me a detailed letter about each member of your family, and your life style," the chaplain had told me over the phone.

Two months later Chaplain Grant had called and spoken with unmistakable enthusiasm, "Mrs. West, I have him! Sorry it took so long, but I had to select one young man in over five hundred! Name's Tommy Bennett. May I come and talk with your family about Tommy this Saturday?"

"Yes, yes," I had exclaimed with delight. After hanging up the phone I repeated, "Tommy Bennett," over and over and I cried a little bit. I asked God to show us some way to help Tommy. I had no idea what our family could do for him or even why I'd wanted to do this.

The chaplain came Saturday morning. Jerry, our four children,

* Real names not used.

and I sat around our kitchen table listening to Chaplain Grant talk about Tommy. "When I told Tommy that your family wanted to—to know him, he said, 'Me? They want to know me?' Then he lit up like a Christmas tree. Tommy works in our prison garage. He's a good mechanic."

We also learned that Tommy was in prison for armed robbery and that he hadn't heard much from his family since he'd been there. The chaplain added, "One reason I selected Tommy is that he seldom complains; he's a hard worker; he's a little shy—and I believe he's the young man God wanted you to have."

Each of us around the table prayed that our family might somehow reach out and help Tommy.

I wrote him immediately, but it wasn't until after I'd written a second letter that I received an answer. Written on notebook paper, the short letter told of his activities and interests. No complaints, nor did he ask anything of us. The letter was reminiscent of one from a dutiful child at camp.

Finally we settled on a date to drive to the prison and meet Tommy. The chaplain said we could come any Saturday or Sunday.

When we got there we had to park a long way from the prison entrance and we'd forgotten our umbrellas. A cold, gray rain came down. We stood in line as our names were checked with those on the official visiting file. The guards let us pass, but the girls and I had to leave our purses along with the gifts we'd brought Tommy at the gate. By the time we located the right building we were shivering and out of breath.

Inside, a guard told us, "Wait outside that door, and after a while Tommy will walk through it. We've called him."

We waited for about thirty minutes, watching each young man appear in the doorway and melt into the arms of a waiting family. I glanced over to the visitation room. It resembled an old train station with bare, scarred walls and "joined-together" type of seats. Litter cluttered the floor. No hint of humor, warmth, or comfort. As we waited, staring at the door Tommy would come through, I became aware that my usually superactive sons were uncommonly silent and still. I was also aware that my heart beat rapidly and I held on to one of the twins' hands with unusual tightness.

*Lord, I'm afraid. Oh, it's so ugly here. Should I have brought our children here? Suppose Tommy doesn't like us? What will we talk about? How can we possibly do anything for him? God, help us.*

Just then Tommy rushed through the door at the end of the hall. I don't know how Jerry and I knew it was Tommy. We just knew. He appeared strong, even though slightly built. Dark hair. Eager eyes. Jerry reached out instantly, offering his hand. Tommy quickly grabbed it, and at the same time gave me his left hand. The three of us just stood there for a silent moment gripping hands and grinning. Then we all talked at once, and introduced Tommy to the children. We headed for the train-terminal-like room to begin our visit. Clearing away some empty drink cans and discarded candy paper, we chose a section of seats over in a corner.

Conversation was easy. Tommy listened, seeming to drink in everything we said. He responded quickly to our questions. His eyes crinkled when he laughed. He laughed often—softly. He told Jon and Jeremy that he liked their new sweaters, and they grinned at each other, then at us. When we went to the canteen to get something to drink, Tommy placed his hand gently on one of the boys' shoulders and sort of guided him along.

He said good things about the prison but agreed that the visiting room needed cleaning. He'd graduated from high school while in prison and now took college courses—wanted to attend the University when he got out. He came up for parole in about a year. There were no uncomfortable silences. Tommy spoke of the "free" world with open admiration, not bitterness.

As our visiting time grew short, Tommy said softly, "I know there's something in life that I haven't found. Something that— holds everything together—something special. I keep thinking I'll find it around the next corner. I *know* I'll find it somewhere, ya know?" His eyes crinkled with anticipation.

Jerry and I nodded. It was time to go. We walked back down the hall with Tommy and touched his shoulder briefly as he went back through the door. "Thank you for coming," he smiled at us. "Drive carefully."

Letters from Tommy came regularly and with less formality. "Dearest Marion, Jerry, Julie, Jen, Jon and Jeremy," they began, closing with "Love ya." Humor crept into the letters as they grew longer and less guarded.

I sent him a box of books and magazines. He sent me essays he'd written in English class. Jon and Jeremy mailed him pictures of cars they'd drawn along with scribbled notes. Tommy sent them colored photographs of cars. The boys took them to school for show-and-tell. And at each meal, they prayed, "God, help Tommy get out of prison."

Before Christmas I carefully followed the instructions I'd been given entitled "Sending Packages to Inmates." They couldn't receive much and only gifts sent through the mail could be accepted. Many items I would have chosen were forbidden. But I selected candies, cookies, warm socks, checkers, pecans—things like that. And I put Christmas stickers on the items, since they couldn't be wrapped. I thought happily, as I mailed the package, we'll get Christmas in to Tommy, even if he is in prison.

Early in January a letter came from Tommy. He wrote that he now had gotten permission to clean up the visiting area and that it looked much better. He joked about the cardboard he'd stuffed into a broken window over his bunk and the snow that blew in on him. Then he wrote with such enthusiasm that his handwriting became almost sketchy:

. . . helped two needy families and a home for the retarded. The home runs on very little funds. An eighty-year-old woman looks after forty persons. We gave her a check for $75 and some turkeys. It's hard to even look at the pictures that were taken. Seeing somebody thirty-one years old in a baby bed—it makes you stop and be thankful for the way you are. One of the families we helped was really very special. They were unable to buy their kids any toys and they had no meat to set on the table. I didn't get to go give the toys and turkeys and groceries to them, but I'm co-chairman of a new project. I'm getting officers and friends who have furniture and household things they don't need in their garages to donate them. It just might work . . .

The last paragraph read:

I enjoyed the card and package y'all sent to me. It really meant something. I'm number one at checkers. Please write me soon. Love ya, Tommy.

I stared at the letter for a long time. Finally I folded it, put it in my desk drawer, and smiled to myself. Christmas had reached Tommy in prison, but not through our package. Tommy found Christmas and a new kind of freedom when he discovered the unique joy of giving. I believed Tommy was well on his way to discovering the joy of learning to lean on Jesus. That was the something in life that he was searching for. I knew it was.

# 30

# THE TOUGH GUY

I continued writing Tommy and sending him books. I mentioned more and more about accepting Jesus in my letters, and I sent him books about people who'd found Jesus.

I had a strong desire to send Tommy some David Wilkerson books. Somehow, I thought this minister could get through to him. I never knew for sure when he received things I sent. Often Tommy would admit that he hadn't gotten a package. I sent Tommy several books, including *The Cross and the Switchblade.*

Time passed and no enthusiastic letter from Tommy arrived. I'd been so sure he'd like David Wilkerson and that Mr. Wilkerson could present Jesus in a way that Tommy would accept.

One Sunday we went to see Tommy on the spur of the moment. It was a warm, sunny day with blue skies—so different from that first visit. Tommy came bounding through the door, and we found a place to sit and talk. The visiting room did look better since Tommy had been cleaning it. Tommy seemed especially talkative. Things were going well for him. "Did you get the books?" I asked right away.

"What books?"

"Oh, Tommy, you didn't get them," I said with disappointment. "I sent you some books, one by someone very special. I just knew you'd like him. A minister named David Wilkerson."

"You're kidding," he grinned.

"No, I sent them."

"Well, I didn't get any books. I got something better."

"Tommy, don't tease. This is serious."

"I'm serious. David Wilkerson was here this week. I met him."

"Here! Tommy, you are teasing. He's very busy. He wouldn't come here."

"Well, he did. We picked it up from the grapevine that he was coming a few days before he came. I didn't know who he was, but I figured I might as well go and hear what he had to say. Didn't have nothing else to do. Almost all the guys went. Man, I've never seen anyone want someone to listen to them so bad in all my life. All he wanted was for us to listen."

"Did you listen?"

"Yeah," he grinned.

"Did you like him?"

"Who could help but like that man?"

Something kept me from asking Tommy if he'd come to know Jesus through hearing Mr. Wilkerson. I hoped he'd tell me, but the boys came up and started asking Tommy questions about cars. I wanted to say, "Tommy, the something you're looking for in life—that's what David Wilkerson was talking about. That's what his life is committed to." But I kept quiet and soon it was time to leave.

"I'll find out the next time we come," I promised myself. I'll come right out and ask Tommy about his relationship with Jesus. We walked to the door with Tommy and said our good-byes. Tommy waved till we were out of sight. He was smiling, too.

A week later I got a call from the chaplain. We'd talked on the phone before about Tommy. But something in the tone of his voice made me uneasy. "Dear Lord," I prayed, "what's happened to Tommy? Has he been hurt in an accident? A riot? Could he be—dead?" Something was terribly wrong.

"Have you heard from Tommy lately?" the chaplain repeated his question.

"No, not since we saw him last week." I didn't know whether to ask questions or just answer his.

There was a long silence. Then the chaplain said, "I have some bad news for you."

Is he hurt or dead, my mind raced ahead.

"Tommy has . . . *escaped!*"

The word seemed to bounce off me. I couldn't accept it. "No, there's some mistake," I thought. The chaplain continued, "He seemed trustworthy. His parole is almost due. He was out on a recreational trip. We allow prisoners like Tommy to do that occasionally. He just walked away. If you hear from him, you'll have to let me know right away." There was a new sternness in his voice.

I sat and stared out the kitchen window. Tommy escaped! Tommy with crinkling eyes that admired my boys' new sweaters. Tommy who helped others at Christmas. Who volunteered to clean up that horrible room and wrote letters signed, "Love ya." A new thought popped into my mind. Suppose he shows up here. He knows our address. He could even approach one of the children. He knows them. I made a firm decision. "I will not live with fear. I refuse it."

I did a lot of thinking. I believed Tommy was about ready to commit his life to Jesus and that Satan had somehow intervened and tempted him. Tommy had yielded to the temptation. I didn't excuse him. He was wrong. I was deeply disappointed in Tommy but not afraid of him.

Weeks and months passed. No one could find a clue. Chaplain Grant called again to ask if I had heard anything. He suspected that Tommy might still be in the state. "We always find them," he assured me. "Tommy is taking a little longer, but we'll find him."

"I want to know when you do. I hope we can see him," I said.

About three months later the doorbell rang early one morning. I'd slept a little later than usual and wasn't fully awake. I opened the door and a large, stern-looking man stood there. He held a card up and said, "I need to ask you some questions."

I squinted in the bright sun and looked at the card. I've never known what you were supposed to look for when someone shows you identification. This was my first time to see a detective's I.D. close up. It looked okay to me.

I asked him inside, and we sat down in the living room. He said right away, "Do you know where Tommy Bennett is?"

"What," I almost hollered, still not fully awake. "How in the world would I know anything about him?"

"He could have contacted you."

"You must be kidding."

"I'm not kidding, Mrs. West," he said grimly. "This is official business. As an investigator, I take my work quite seriously. Tommy has evaded us longer than anyone who has ever escaped from that prison. Will you answer some questions for me?"

"Of course." I was wide awake now.

He got out a small notebook and said, "Exactly why did you make contact with him in the first place?"

I looked at the tough, staunch man and thought, will you understand? "We wanted to help him," I answered. "We just asked for a prisoner—any prisoner—and we got Tommy."

He looked at me for a moment, started to say something, then changed his mind and wrote and said aloud, "Civic responsibility."

I hated his answer. I tried to let it pass, but I couldn't. I said, "It wasn't civic responsibility. We are Christians, and we wanted to help him—know God."

He marked through his answer fast and hard with his pen. I couldn't see what he wrote. "Maybe 'Nuts,'" I thought.

He looked at me again. Then he seemed to notice a praying hands statue on the coffee table.

"You sound like my wife."

I brightened.

"She's Pentecostal. Are you?"

"No, but we're still the same. Churches don't make that much difference. I wish I knew her."

"You sure sound like her. Guess you go to church all the time too, don't you?"

"Yes, just up the street.

"Sir," I asked suddenly, "are you a Christian?"

"Let's get back to our questions." He began asking me various things once more and wrote down my answers. He cautioned, "You wouldn't try to reason with Tommy or anything if he called you, would you? You wouldn't see him. He could be dangerous."

Tommy dangerous? All I could see were his twinkling eyes and I could hear him say, "There's something in life that holds everything together. I'm looking for it."

"No, I won't try to reason with him. My husband has already told me not to do that."

"Good. Is there anything else you want to say?"

"Do you think I know something that I'm not telling you?" I asked flatly.

He shook his head. "No, you tell the truth . . . because you're . . ."

"A Christian?" I laughed a little.

He nodded, almost smiled, and said, "Well, you sure got taken trying to do good. Tommy fooled you."

"I don't feel taken."

"Well, you were! You must admit now that you got the wrong prisoner. You ended up with one who escaped."

"Seems like he was the exact prisoner we were supposed to have. Five hundred men and only one has escaped and you can't find him. Pretty good to have someone praying for him, don't you think?"

"But you're so gullible, you do-gooders. You believe anything and love everybody." He said it without malice, just exasperation.

I didn't know what to say. I could hardly believe my words: "Sir, in your job, don't you ever get to the place where you feel like you just can't do it anymore on your own? Don't you ever need to ask Jesus for help?"

He put his pen in his pocket, closed his little black book, and looked at me for a moment. Then he spoke—in a different tone of voice. He looked down. He didn't seem so big or stern or tough now.

"Yes, yes, yes! I need Him fifty times a day, *every day*. I need Him."

My heart leaped. "Then why don't you just invite—"

He stopped me. "I can't become a Christian. I can't ever do that. I can't ever be naive like you and go around loving everybody. My business is a tough one and I have to be tough. I *am* tough."

"Jesus had more guts than any man who ever lived. Being a Christian takes guts too. It's not for sissies." I said it gently and without any tone of argument in my voice. I hurt for him.

For a wild moment, I thought he was going to accept Christ in my living room! His jaw flinched and he stood up suddenly to his full height, about six feet four inches. He was professional again. "Thank you for answering the questions. Here's my card. If you learn anything about Tommy, phone me immediately."

I took the card. He started out the door and I said, "I hope I didn't say anything that . . ."

He turned and smiled very slightly. "No, it's all right. The woman

I had to question before I came here blessed me out. Called me every name in the book. This was a nice change of pace."

He left quickly.

Several years have passed. I haven't heard from Tommy or the man who is looking for him. I pray for both of them, a young, escaped convict who is looking for Something to hold things together, and a tough investigator: two men with the same desperate need.

# 31

# YES, MY JULIE*

I awakened in the middle of the night, my mouth dry and tears stinging my eyes. The dream seemed still to be in the room with me. My heart pounded. I crawled out of bed and made my way down the dark hall to Julie's room. I stood in the doorway looking at her for a moment in the moonlight. She slept sprawled in her bed with the covers untucked like a seven-year-old, instead of a seventeen-year-old.

I slipped back into my bed. The dream stayed in my mind. I'd been talking to a doctor in a hospital. We were communicating well, smiling and nodding. There were bright yellow curtains around us—the kind that are often in hospital rooms separating patients. (Yellow curtains had also been in the labor room when Julie was born.) Suddenly the doctor said matter-of-factly—he smiled too—"You understand that Julie is leaving us. She's not going to make it. You must give her up now."

"What!" I had screamed until my throat ached, hating the mild-mannered man for talking so calmly about giving up Julie. "No, I don't know anything of the kind. She's fine. I don't have to give her up. I'll show you." I jerked the yellow curtain back with all my strength. Julie was behind it in a hospital bed. I've seen two people that I loved near death. One died, one recovered. Julie looked identical to them. I screamed, "No, my Julie. Nooooo."

When I woke up I could still hear my screams and taste the anguish in my dry mouth. I determined not to go over the dream in my mind again. "Lord, help me sleep now," I prayed. I drifted back to sleep, and the dream faded somewhat. In the morning it seemed to live in a tiny corner of my mind.

I told Jerry about the dream while he brushed his teeth. I wanted someone to say, "That's silly. Forget it." He said just that. The memory of the dream shrank some more, but occasionally I thought about it. "Lord, I must not dwell on this. Help me forget it."

* Reprinted by permission of *Guideposts* magazine, Copyright 1980 by Guideposts Associates, Inc., Carmel, New York 10512.

By Christmas I'd practically forgotten all about it. Busy days came one on top of the other. They rolled by hurriedly, like a movie that had been speeded up.

Three days before Christmas Julie's boyfriend's mother said she wanted to come by and bring us some cookies she'd baked. We'd gotten to know each other pretty well. I was a little in awe of Carolyn, however. She was an excellent cook, fantastic house-keeper, could work wonders arranging flowers, and knew how to keep the books where her husband worked. She never got in a hurry and did things with perfection. Once Julie told me, "Mother, there's not even one speck of dust under her sofa. I looked. It shines under there." I'd been overcome by her bathrooms. They looked just like the ones in home magazines.

Carolyn came in and greeted my mother, who was visiting with us, then me. The three of us sat and talked for over an hour. We talked about Julie and Ricky and Christmas. It was a good visit. I appreciated Carolyn's coming over.

Then she got up to leave and looked right at me and said, "Marion, there's something I have to tell you, and I might as well not beat around the bush about it." My mother nearly fell up the den steps, running, so we two could talk alone.

I smiled and said, "Certainly." But I wasn't smiling on the inside. A hint of what she was about to say had already touched my pounding heart.

"Do you know that Ricky is giving Julie a ring for Christmas? An engagement ring?"

"No," I said calmly, while my heart hammered loudly and I felt slightly sick to my stomach.

"I didn't think you suspected. I went with him to pick out the ring a few days ago. Julie doesn't know she's getting it, and she can't seem to talk to you about—their plans."

My voice remained calm; I said something. The shock was apparent, I'm sure.

"I had to tell you," she said. "It wasn't easy."

"Thank you," I said. "Thank you so much for coming." I couldn't smile. My heart felt like a meat hammer was clawing away at it. I saw Carolyn to the door and, as she drove off, the dream I'd almost forgotten mushroomed back to its original size and inside I screamed silently, "No, my Julie. Noooo." The time had come to give up Julie. Engaged at seventeen, married at eighteen.

"*No.*"

Mother came downstairs and said, "You look just like you did when you found out you were having twins."

"Julie's getting a diamond."

My mother smiled. "Didn't you think she might? Didn't it occur to you? Have you watched them together?"

"I didn't suspect," I answered. "I knew someday—but someday shouldn't be here yet." The ache in my heart grew to tremendous proportions while I fixed supper, answered the phone, and wrapped Christmas gifts. It was Julie's last Christmas at home. I kept seeing her as a baby, crawling to the Christmas tree; a toddler learning to swim, to ride a bike, cheering at ballgames.

"No, my Julie."

I remembered the day she'd brought Ricky in to meet me. He rode the school bus home with her. She was just fourteen. He was her first (and only) boyfriend. I think I knew the first time I saw him that they would be married someday. Ricky was quiet, gentle, and easy to love. He was also a Christian.

Since Julie didn't know she was getting the ring, there was nothing I could say. Unless, of course, Jerry and I decided not to let her accept it. He'd remained absolutely quiet when I told him. He seemed to look beyond me. I'd only seen that look on his face a few times in our twenty years of marriage.

We'd naturally assumed Julie would go to school for four years somewhere. She was a straight-A student.

Jerry's eyes met mine and, without saying a word, we both knew that we couldn't refuse to support Julie and Ricky. We would give them our blessings.

Walking down the stairs, I prayed, "Lord, help me. I can't do this. Help me."

I thought back to a recent conversation as Julie and I had looked at college brochures. Panic had seemed to fill her face and voice. "Mother, I just want one thing . . . to be a Christian wife and mother. I don't want a career. I want to stay at home and bake cakes and play with my children and cook for my husband."

"That will come," I had said and showed her another brochure.

"Look at this one. This is where they are offering you a partial scholarship. Looks nice, doesn't it?"

She'd looked politely and nodded. Julie had never done one thing to displease us.

Her daddy had told her, "You pick out a school, and we'll go see it one day soon. You just pick out one."

I remembered also that several times I'd found her crying. Unusual for Julie. She'd hardly cried even as a child. She never complained. I should have taken her tears more seriously.

Christmas Eve, Julie and Ricky decided to exchange gifts at his house. I tried to imagine the scene while I waited for them to come to our house. Finally, I heard them coming in the front door. I went up the den steps and they stood in the kitchen together, right where they had stood the first day Julie had brought him to our home. She had her hands behind her back. Mother, knowing what tonight held for her, had bought her a beautiful new outfit and given it to her early. She wore it.

They just stood there silently with a sort of glow around them. I'd never seen her smile like this. I tried to recall some bad decisions she'd made in the past. There had been only one that I could remember. It seemed strange, but I remembered it now, of all times. She bought some horrible green shoes, and I told her they were ridiculous and would hurt her feet. She wore them only three times. I had been right.

But her other decisions had been good, solid. Many of them based on prayer. Pretty good record, one pair of wrong shoes.

Mother, Jerry, Jennifer, the boys, and I gathered around Julie and Ricky. She held out her hand. There it was! Sure enough—a lovely diamond on her finger. The ring blurred as my eyes brimmed with tears for a moment. And I saw instead a little hand making mud pies, tiny fingers cutting out paperdolls, and youthful hands that had learned to play the piano.

I blinked my eyes and said, "It's beautiful, Julie." Her daddy hugged her, so did my mother, finally I did.

We took pictures of them and no one had to say, "Smile now." They couldn't stop smiling.

The wedding would be a year from Christmas, next December 9. Julie wanted to attend a local college for a year and then work for a doctor. Ricky was already attending the same college and working. They would be out for Christmas holidays on the ninth.

Christmas day, Julie told me that the first thing they wanted for their home was a family Bible. "You know, a big one that you can hardly lift." I knew what she wanted and was overjoyed with her request.

I wanted to run right out and buy the Bible, but I knew they were quite expensive and right after Christmas we couldn't afford it. I told Jerry about Julie and Ricky wanting the Bible and he smiled. "We'll get them one," he said.

The day after Christmas, Jerry said a shirt I had given him just wasn't his style and asked me to go with him to exchange it. I was busy, and it hurt my feelings because he wanted to swap it, so I didn't really want to go.

But I felt a prodding to go. For some reason the Lord wanted me to go with Jerry. I said yes. We exchanged the shirt and were walking to the car. A store that sold old books had moved into the shopping center. Knowing how I love books, Jerry entered. We looked around for a while, then separated. When I found Jerry once again, he was bent over, looking closely at a book. He held it up for me to see. It wasn't used—it was brand-new. It was a large, ivory Bible and it was lovely. He pointed to the price—half the original price of $25.00 because of a scratch on the binding. The owner of the store saw us looking at it and said, "You two can have it for eight."

We had six dollars' change from the exchanged shirt. We didn't say anything. We just looked at the Bible. "Make it four," the owner said with apparent joy. "You people really seem to appreciate that book."

Jerry paid for it, and we didn't let her wrap it. We walked down the sidewalk and read from it as we walked. The illustrations were breathtaking. Finally, we just stood still and read from it. People walked around us and stared openly.

It didn't matter. The first thing that Julie and Ricky wanted in their home was this Bible. The Lord had directed us to it and, somehow, it was like ointment on a wound to me. Joy began to grow in my heart. I expected a lot more of it.

We bought paper and wrapped the Bible as a wedding gift and gave it to Julie and Ricky as soon as we got home. They opened it together and looked in silent awe. I knew Julie wondered how we afforded it just after Christmas. After they thanked us, they took it to show to Ricky's parents.

As they drove off I remembered her words: "All I want is to be a Christian wife and mother."

All? All! That was everything!

On Mother's Day, May 14, 1978, Julie gave me a lovely card and a gift that must have cut way into her paycheck. (She worked for a vet.) The card had a beautiful printed message on it. I've forgotten what it said, but I've almost memorized the note Julie wrote on the card:

Mother, what I've always heard about mothers and never believed before, I am now finding to be true . . . the older I get, the more I appreciate and understand you. Since this will be my last Mother's Day at home . . . I have really been thinking about my life at home so far. It's the little things you've done that come to my mind, like bringing my books to school that I forgot so many times, taking me to "umpteen" practices, making asparagus casseroles at the last minute, and helping me make posters. But more important is how you have taught me about life. You have been honest with me with everything, and I think I appreciate that the most. You always answered my questions, from "Why is the sky blue?" to "Where do babies come from?" I have often tried to figure out where I would be spiritually if I hadn't been brought up in a Christian home. When I was listening to you speak at the mother-daughter banquet, I really realized how fortunate I am to have a Christian mother (not everyone does, you know). I know I turned out "okay" and it wasn't any of my doing. Maybe it was the "gold cadillac."* I just hope and pray I will have the wisdom,

* AUTHOR'S NOTE: When Julie was nineteen months we got her a little car for Christmas—a "gold cadillac." Her legs barely reached the pedals. One day she tried to back it up, and couldn't understand to turn the wheel left if she wanted to go right. I explained to her how to do it, but of course a child that young couldn't understand. I spanked her and raised my voice. Years later, I remembered the incident and apologized. She smiled and said she remembered it quite well. "I also learned how to back that car up. You expected too much of me, and I was determined to do what you wanted. I think since that day I set high goals for myself. Thanks."

guts and maturity and love to be able to bring up my children as you have reared me. Thank you. Julie.

Looking at the card, I smiled, cried, and smiled some more. Only one thought came to my mind. It completely blocked out my previous thoughts of "No, my Julie."

I thought happily, even though I was amazed that I could do it, "Yes, my Julie. Yes. You've made the right decision. You're going to be a fine Christian wife and mother. God bless you both."

# 32

## CROWN HIM THE KING OF KINGS

For several years my dentist had been telling me that eventually I'd have to have a couple of my back teeth crowned. Eventually seemed like a long time away. After each checkup I'd ease gratefully out of his chair. He hadn't said, "Right away."

When I chewed on a jawbreaker that one of my boys had given me shortly after my last visit to the dentist, a large portion of one of my back teeth broke off. I brooded about it for several days. Crowns were expensive. I became obsessed by how much it would cost to have the tooth fixed. I didn't call the dentist.

Somewhere in the back of my mind, I knew that worrying about the cost wasn't an expression of trust in the Lord. But I continued to worry, silently, of course. For almost a week this went on. I read in my Bible how we shouldn't be anxious about anything and the more I read, the more anxious I became. Because one of the children had just had dental surgery and we were planning Julie's wedding, I just didn't see how a crown for my tooth could work into our budget. I continued to fret about the situation.

Then a second tooth broke when I was eating another piece of candy. I could have cried—but instead I started laughing and prayed, "I just can't worry about two teeth, Lord. This is too much for me. I could barely manage to handle all the worry about one. I just can't handle two!" I had this funny feeling for a moment that if I kept worrying my teeth might just keep breaking, one by one.

I phoned the dentist for an appointment. The price of the two crowns would be three hundred and fifty dollars.

Jerry told me to have the work done and stop mumbling about it. He said to take the money out of savings. But I couldn't get away from the idea that the Lord would supply the money. After all, the Bible says that we have not because we ask not. If the Lord knew the numbers of hairs on my head, surely He knew about my teeth too.

I decided that maybe our insurance would pay for the teeth,

even though Jerry said it wouldn't. The dentist thought it would. I felt very spiritual sitting in the chair with my mouth wide open. I could just see that insurance check coming in. The Lord would supply my needs.

After the work was completed, I waited in anticipation for the check to arrive. The word came back quickly. They couldn't pay it, nor were they supposed to. A cordial letter of explanation accompanied the rejected insurance claim.

With great disappointment I got the money out of savings and wondered why my prayer hadn't been answered. I finally decided that it was foolish of me to think I could pray about crowns. I'd almost forgotten the incident when a friend related an experience to me and I saw my great error.

Five of us were having lunch at my house. We were all Christians, and I knew the conversation would center around what the Lord was teaching each of us. At the last minute I pulled five scriptures from a little box of "Daily Bread" and placed one at everyone's place. After we finished eating, I would ask my friends to read their scripture and, if it related to anything in their lives, to share it with us. I'd selected the scriptures at random, hardly reading them. Because I had placed an arrangement of orange and red zinnias on the table, I wanted all orange scriptures. They came in five colors.

As we read our scriptures, I thought it strange that Dawn and I got the same one. I had no idea there were two of any of the scriptures. She read hers: "Behold, the Lord's hand is not shortened, that it cannot save; neither his ear heavy, that it cannot hear" (Isaiah 59:1, KJV). She smiled to herself for a moment, like she was trying to make up her mind whether to share her thoughts or not. Finally she said, "Well, this makes me remember what the Lord has just done for us. You all know that when we *really* found Jesus a few years ago, it changed our life-styles a great deal. We got rid of a large home and many antiques." (I'd seen pictures of the beautiful Victorian home they once lived in. I also knew because their income as staff workers with Campus Crusade for Christ would be much less than they had been accustomed to, that they had gotten rid of a lot of their furniture as well as the house.) Dawn continued: "There were quite a few antiques that we wanted my mother to have. All these years she's had them. I guess it's been about nine years."

She smiled again. "This is sort of complicated. Hang in there with me. I've had some teeth that the dentist has told me for years had to be crowned before they gave me real trouble and I had to have root canals."

I was really hanging in there, listening.

She continued: "Last visit to him, he said I couldn't wait any longer. I had to have *five* crowned, plus our daughter had to have braces. We didn't have that kind of money, but I knew that the Lord knew our needs better than I did and that He was faithful to provide. *I didn't worry at all about the money.*"

I was sitting on the edge of my chair. "Didn't worry *at all,*" I thought. "Good grief!" Would the Lord work out the money situation for *five* crowns? Dawn had said that she wasn't about to even try to figure out how He would do it. She said that wasn't her business.

She continued with the story: "I had a little money I'd received for speaking to Christian Women's Club, but the Lord had already told me what to do with that money. I was to send two young women that I'd taught in my Sunday school class to The Basic Youth Conflict.* I knew they couldn't afford to go if someone didn't pay their way. They didn't want me to do it at first. But I told them that the Lord would redeem the hundred dollars. He always had, and I was excited about giving them the money. So I finally talked them into letting me send them to the seminar.

"Now, back to the antiques." Dawn laughed. "My mother's house was broken into recently, and the robbers took the antiques that we'd given Mother nine years ago. The insurance adjuster called Mother the other day and said our appraisal was quite conservative. So, to make a long story short, we're getting a check for two thousand dollars! We'll have money left over. God is faithful," Dawn said softly, her eyes brimming with tears.

I've thought about her crowns a lot. It's become quite clear to me

---

* A week's course taught each year by Bill Gothard in cities. The principles he teaches usually have dramatic effects in changing people's lives. Thousands attend.

that I didn't put my problems of finance in God's hands. I'd tried to help Him. I also knew that if I had had one hundred dollars, I wouldn't have sent those girls to Bill Gothard. Not with that dental bill facing me. It just wouldn't have been reasonable to give it away then. But reason had caused me to stumble before when trying to trust the Lord.

There also seems to be a principle involved of giving out of your need, not surplus. Something the Lord's been trying to teach me for quite a while.

I thought happily as I cleaned up the kitchen after my friends had gone, "God does care about teeth after all!" My approach and attitude had been wrong. I can ask Him for anything, but there are prerequisites that must be followed. Even with my three-hundred-and-fifty-dollar dental bill just paid, I rejoiced that the King of Kings and Lord of Lords never changes. Answers to prayer must come according to His Word—His way—never pushing or prompting Him but trusting *completely* and leaning on Him for a solution.

# 33

## PLEASE HOLD MY HAND*

I felt helpless as my daughter shared her fear with me. Rules were rules, and I didn't see how I could change them.

I listened, but it seemed hopeless. "Mother, I know I have to have the surgery and I know it isn't serious. I really want to get these impacted wisdom teeth out. I don't like to put things off. I don't mind going in the hospital if the doctor thinks that's best. But you know what will happen when they get me down to the operating room."

I nodded. I knew from the two previous minor surgeries Julie had experienced during the past several years. She would put on a brave front, smile, make polite conversation to anyone who spoke to her, and go to surgery without any complaints. Then down in the operating room as she was waiting to be put to sleep—there was always the wait—she'd shake. Not tremble mildly, but shake so violently that she'd be sore from the shaking.

"Mother, I dread the shaking more than the surgery or the pain. I'm eighteen years old, engaged to be married, and I shake so hard I rattle the bars on the bed."

"We can pray about it," I suggested. We always prayed before Julie's surgery, but we'd never prayed about the shaking. During the next few days before she entered the hospital, we began to pray that somehow she wouldn't shake.

I got to the hospital on the morning of surgery early only to learn that she wouldn't go to surgery until twelve fifteen.

"Did you sleep well?" I asked hopefully.

"No, I kept waking up and thinking about shaking. And I started to shake just thinking about it." I sat by the bed, and Julie reached for my hand. About ten thirty a nurse came and gave Julie a pre-op shot. It relaxed her a little, but she stayed wide awake. I noticed that her legs had begun to tremble. I sat on the bed and put my

* Reprinted by permission of *Guideposts* magazine, Copyright 1979 by Guideposts Associates, Inc., Carmel, New York 10512.

hand on her legs. Finally, I almost lay across them. I couldn't stop the shaking.

"Mother, ask them to let you come to the operating room with me and hold my hand. That's all I need . . . just till I go to sleep."

"I don't think they'll let me, but I'll ask. I have one other suggestion." From my purse I pulled out a small card. When I'd been searching through my desk drawer for stamps one day, the smiling face of a little girl on a card had seemed to look right up at me. She had red hair like Julie and was saying, "Hi, just wanted to tell you that . . ." The rest of the message had been on the inside of the greeting card. I'd cut the part of the card off that just showed the adorable little girl whispering her message. There was plenty of space for me to write in my own message. I wrote, "I need someone to hold my hand while I'm waiting to be put to sleep. I won't shake if you'll hold my hand. Thanks, Julie."

I read the note to her and added, "If you'll let me, I'll tape this note to your sheet. Someone will see it in the operating room. See, I even remembered to bring Scotch tape."

"They'll think I'm a baby," Julie said softly.

I didn't comment. Julie still shook. She sighed and said, "All right. If you can't go with me, put the note on the sheet."

Just then a woman came to take Julie to surgery. I helped Julie tuck her long hair under the small green cap. And I asked the woman, "Could I possibly go along and stay till she goes to sleep?" I knew the answer before I asked.

She smiled, "No, I'm sorry. You can go only as far as the doors to the operating room. Rules."

I smiled back at her. "I understand. I'll just go down on the elevator with you." I quickly taped the card onto Julie's sheet and the woman and I rolled her down the hall. At the doors of the operating room, I read Julie's lips, "I love you." I kissed her on the forehead and waved good-bye.

In just twenty-five minutes the doctor phoned me in her room to say that she was in recovery and would be back in the room in about forty-five minutes. He said surgery had gone beautifully.

When they brought Julie back, her eyes were open and she was smiling the best she could with the gauze pads sticking out of her mouth and the ice pack tied around her head. She winked and made an "okay sign" by putting her thumb and forefinger together in a circle. As soon as they got her into bed and left, she began waving her wrist around in the air to get my attention.

Finally I figured out the motion. She couldn't talk and wanted to write. I handed her a pad and pen. Still groggy, she scribbled, "I have to see the black lady that came to get me. She's wonderful. Read your note and wrapped me in warm sheets and patted me on shoulder and talked to me. Never left me. She held my hand all the time! I went to sleep with her holding my hand and smiling at me. Please get her up here."

When I promised I would, Julie immediately went to sleep.

Later in the day, I asked one of the aides if the woman from the operating room could stop by Julie's room. She didn't know which woman I meant. I described her as best I could. "She smiles a lot," I added.

"Oh, that's Ernestine. I'll ask her to come by."

Ernestine came in flashing a warm smile. I showed her the note from Julie. Even with the gauze pads in her mouth Julie managed to say, "Thank you." Ernestine brushed off my attempts of profound gratitude and talked instead about Julie's pretty red hair.

When the doctor came by that evening, he asked me right away, "Did you put that note on Julie?"

Not sure of what he was going to say, I admitted that I had.

His stern face broke into a big grin and he said, "Well, that was about the neatest thing we've ever seen in the operating room. We want to help people. Often we just don't know what their fears are. Ernestine stayed right with Julie. I wish more people would tell us their fears and how we can help them. We really like to help people."

After he left, I sat back down and looked out the window at the panoramic view of the city. I could see people moving in all directions, both walking and in cars. I wondered how many of them harbored an unspoken fear. Perhaps many of their fears could be resolved by a quiet act, like someone holding their hand.

I knew that many people, myself included, had endured hidden fears because of pride. As I watched Julie sleep, my heart filled with gratitude. She'd had the courage to admit to strangers her desperate need, *Please hold my hand,* and the Lord had provided Ernestine.

# 34

# I WILL LIFT UP MINE EYES
# UNTO THE HILLS

Because of our hectic schedules and not wanting to leave Julie, who couldn't get away from her job, and the extra medical expenses we'd experienced during the summer, we decided not to take our annual family vacation. It suited me fine. I don't like to ride, pack or unpack, and caring for everyone who gets sunburned at the beach isn't my idea of fun. Neither is making countless sandwiches for someone who's always hungry. I was secretly happy that we were staying at home this year. No one seemed to mind much, except Jerry. He likes to plan our routes on maps, get up early in the morning and figure out how to get all the luggage in the car, and then drive all day. At the beach he even likes the kiddy parks and boardwalks, which I can't stand. I like isolation, and commercialism of any kind bothers me. He loves seafood, and I'm allergic to most of it. He swims way out in the ocean and then floats on his back, and I stay near the shore because I don't like fish swimming around my feet. He goes out on the pier and fishes. I went with him one day and quickly ran back to the shore. All the dead and dying fish upset me, and I nearly threw up. He goes deep-sea fishing, and I get motion sickness.

So it definitely wasn't a big deal to me that we were staying at home—except for one thing. I missed the break in our schedule. Our days were too jam-packed. Often Jerry and I saw each other only ten minutes a day. We talked of making some changes, but there was never time. I was leaving him notes, and he'd check answers to my questions. When we tried to talk for a few minutes, children seemed to surround us with fifty or more questions. I go to bed early, he stays up late. When I wanted to talk to him he seemed to be working on a report connected with his work, watching a ballgame on television or cutting the grass.

Mopping the kitchen floor one day, I prayed, "Lord, we need a day and a night away. Just twenty-four hours. Just Jerry and me.

Could You work that out? I mean, I know You could, but would You give me the faith to believe it. We need a break. We've got to have it. I don't know where we could go, not anywhere expensive." Suddenly I remembered a friend of mine who asked the Lord for a mini-vacation, and the next day a friend offered them her beach house for several days. "Could we have something like You gave Charlotte and Al, Lord? Just twenty-four hours?"

I began smiling as I mopped. I somehow believed He would do it! I felt certain that the wheels were already turning so that Jerry and I could have a twenty-four-hour break in our schedule. I thanked the Lord.

Then my boys came in and started to walk on the wet floor and I told them to go to the side door and forgot all about my prayer. I thought instead about how children always come in the minute you mop or wax a floor.

I had just started cooking supper that evening when the phone rang. Someone I didn't know asked me to speak. She said she lived in Jasper, Georgia. I waited for her to finish, so I could say no. I'd accepted too many invitations lately, and knew I couldn't handle any more. Already that day, I'd told two callers that I was sorry but that I couldn't accept. They'd understood.

This caller didn't seem to understand. I explained that I didn't have a good sense of direction and couldn't come by myself and I almost never accepted evening invitations out of town. I didn't know anyone who would come with me to Jasper.

She started telling me how to get to Jasper.

I was about to become exasperated when she explained, "Marion, I don't know anything about you. I've never read anything you've written except the excerpt in *Guideposts*. It wasn't my idea to call you. Several of the women here in our fellowship believe the Lord wants you to come for a two-way ministry."

I listened.

"We think that maybe you and Jerry might like to just—get away for a day and a night. Bent Tree (a beautiful resort area) is located here, and we want you to stay at a villa we'll reserve for you. Just give us a couple of hours to speak the day you get here. Then we'll leave you two completely alone. We have speakers come once a month. It's beautiful here—right near the mountains—just an hour and a half from Atlanta. I don't know why you're supposed to come, but don't say no until you talk with Jerry and pray."

I was stunned. The Lord was answering my prayer and I was refusing. "Yes, yes, of course. I'll talk to Jerry, pray, and call you back."

"Let's pray now," she suggested. She prayed over the phone with me about the decision and she prayed for my family.

Jerry said that he wanted to go and that he could take a day off. I marked the date on my calendar that Marilyn had invited me for. My mother agreed to stay with our children. She wouldn't even let me prepare food for them in advance. "We'll eat out. You and Jerry have a good time."

The day we were to leave, Julie came in from work and handed me a large pink package. "Happy twenty-four-hour vacation, Mama." She beamed and handed me the gift.

"It's not my birthday."

"I know, but you just had to have this."

I opened the lovely package and there in the tissue paper was the most elegant gown and matching negligee in my favorite color, brown. It was trimmed with ivory lace. "Oh, Julie, you can't afford this. You should have it. You're the one getting married. You should have this."

I stopped raving long enough to look at her. A look of pure delight was on her face. "You've been married *twenty years*, and I want you to have it."

Looking at Julie's face, I received the gift. It was exactly what I would have picked out.

Jerry and I got off with the children and Mother standing in the driveway like we were headed for Europe, instead of Jasper, Georgia, an hour and a half away in the foothills of the Georgia mountains.

We were to meet Marilyn and Norm James at a place called the Woodbridge Inn in Jasper. From the minute we arrived in the tiny town, the hurried feeling inside me that I'd been fighting for months evaporated. People moved slowly. Waved. There were rocking chairs on front porches of stores. When the red light changed to green, cars didn't move in a hurry and no one blew their horn. There was only one red light. We spotted the Woodbridge Inn. It looked like something out of a picture book, or *Ideals*. To get to the Inn we had to cross a little, humped bridge. I fought back the desire to look under the bridge for a Billy-goat Gruff.

The Inn was a very old two-story house with a front porch. Geraniums and other plants flourished. The yard was swept clean except for a few patches of grass. Two ageless oak trees shaded the inn. Old school desks and rocking chairs were on the front porch. "We don't even have to eat," I thought wildly. "We can just sit on this wonderful porch and look at the mountains." Jerry reacted the same way I did. We almost never liked the same kind of places, but here we were both awed and grateful.

A young couple came out the door and down the steps to greet us. We knew without introductions that they were Marilyn and Norm James. We hugged, and it seemed natural. Inside we looked at the small gift shop where items made by local people were for sale. I bought gifts for the children and Mother. Norm and Marilyn seemed to know every single person eating in the Inn. Most of them were local people. Almost everyone spoke to them, and stopped eating and spoke to us warmly when we were introduced.

The menu looked wonderful. The Inn was run by a man from Germany and his wife. I quickly realized from looking at the food that was being served that cooking was much more than a business to the owner. It was an art—a way of life.

When our food came, we joined hands and Norm prayed.

Then they took us to our villa at Bent Tree. I hadn't expected much more than a rustic cabin. The villa was secluded and built "into" the woods. Almost no trees had been cut away. It looked like a place that Heidi and her grandfather would have liked. The inside was simply elegant. I hadn't expected that. Plush furnishings, a rock fireplace, carpeting, and ultramodern kitchen, two bedrooms, two and a half baths, and an upstairs and downstairs, plus two patios—just for the two of us! The upper patio was nestled in the treetops. Squirrels and birds were at eye level. Beyond the treetops were the mountains.

I was speechless. Marilyn explained that some of the girls had fixed snacks and they were in the refrigerator. We peeked in. I marveled over the food that had been prepared for us and the clean, spanking new refrigerator. Marilyn said she'd be back around six to pick me up for the meeting.

After they left, Jerry and I stood in the middle of the living room looking out at the mountains. We weren't used to this much privacy or time on our hands. The quietness was beautiful. We walked through the villa and admired it in detail. Then we put on our bathing suits. The pool was within walking distance. We decided to sit out on the patio, the one up in the trees, and admire the view. I fixed us a Coke, and I went out first by myself. When Jerry came out, he shut the door and immediately we both had the same thought. Had we locked ourselves out? He'd taken off the lock, and I, trying to take it off, had simply locked it back.

I started laughing. I laughed so hard, I sat down in a chair. I'd asked the Lord for time alone with Jerry, and it sure looked like He was giving it to me. Jerry started laughing too. He sat down and we laughed out loud. Our laughter echoed across the mountains. We scared away a few birds. It felt wonderful to be locked out on a patio, up in the trees, with my husband. *Thank You, Lord.*

After a while, we decided we had better holler for help. We hollered and hollered. Boy, were we alone! Jerry crawled up on the patio table and started to climb on the roof, but it was so hot he could hardly touch it, and we were both barefoot. I laughed some more, until I saw Jerry had stopped laughing, so I tried to look serious.

In the unbelievable quietness, we heard a vehicle rumbling down the winding road. Then it stopped and a door slammed. "Help," we hollered.

A voice bellowed, "Where are you?"

"On the patio," Jerry called out. "Come through the front door. It's unlocked." In a few moments the smiling face of a construction worker peeped through the patio door and in another second we were free.

We sat by the pool for a couple of hours, then went back so I could dress for the meeting. Jerry planned to explore while I was gone.

At the meeting I watched Marilyn. I'd never seen anyone so aware of people and their needs. She greeted everyone and never seemed to stop smiling. She reached out to touch people often and listen to their problems. The Lord shone through her smile in a marvelous way. Her prayers were to a God whom she knew well and depended on totally.

After the meeting she brought me back to the villa.

We weren't supposed to see Norm and Marilyn anymore, but Jerry wanted to invite them to join us for lunch at the Woodbridge Inn the next day. We phoned them early the next morning, and they planned to meet us at noon. Marilyn wanted to be sure that we weren't just being nice. I finally convinced her that we really wanted to spend some more time with them.

At the Inn, Jerry finally got around to asking Norm what he did. Norm smiled slightly and said, "Oh, I'm a minister down at the Chapel." Jerry smiled and nodded. I knew what the smile meant. *It doesn't show. You don't come on like a minister.* It was a compliment of the highest sort. People kept waving to Norm and coming by our table to speak. When I asked Marilyn if they all went to their church, she said they didn't. Many of them weren't even believers. A few of them were brand-new Christians. I couldn't tell from the way Norm spoke to them which were the believers and which were the nonbelievers. He seemed comfortable with everyone, and they all seemed to like him.

Saying good-bye to our new friends was somewhat more difficult than I'd imagined. We stood outside the car near the bridge and looked silently at the mountains that surrounded us. I thought of the scripture in Psalms 121 that says, "I will lift up mine eyes unto the hills, from whence cometh my help" (KJV). Jerry said, "We'll have to come back."

"Yes," Marilyn agreed. "The Lord has put us together for some purpose. Come back. Soon," she added.

We hugged once again. I was ready to go home. I was rested spiritually and physically. Time hadn't been a factor on this vacation. We were renewed, so renewed, there was no need to talk about it. Both Jerry and I knew something special had happened to us because of Marilyn and Norm.

We drove out of the quaint, little town, past the tiny, new church that said, "The Chapel—Pastor, Norman James." The little church looked like a picture postcard sitting snugly in the midst of the magnificent mountains that surrounded it.

As we drove, I remembered that Marilyn had told me that an old dog, hungry and abandoned, had made his way to the Chapel. People had given him love and food. Someone named the dog Jeremiah. He sat at the entrance of the church and greeted everyone who came. His head was held erect now and his tail was no longer tucked between his legs. It wagged with the joy that comes from acceptance and love. I had a feeling that many of the people who attended the Chapel were grateful to belong also. They too had come hungry and perhaps with a feeling of abandonment.

Driving home, Jerry and I were quiet for miles at a time. Then we would talk about Marilyn and Norm, the Chapel, Bent Tree, Woodbridge Inn, and Jeremiah, and of God's goodness.

I commented to Jerry, "Oh, I forgot to ask Marilyn about her back. I kept hearing people asking her about it. When I did, she said she'd tell me later. I never asked again. Maybe she sprained it or something."

When Marilyn phoned a few days later, just before we hung up I remembered her back problem and asked about it.

There was a brief silence, then her bright voice explained, without groping for words and without one ounce of self-pity, "I have advanced cancer. I've had a mastectomy, but the cancer is back, quite spread, and sometimes my back gives me a little trouble. The doctors have told me to concentrate on quality of life rather than quantity." She spoke smoothly and easily.

I ached suddenly deep inside, and my eyes brimmed with hot, stinging tears. But I resolved that if Marilyn could talk about cancer in that easy tone of voice, that I too would—somehow. I'd sort out my thoughts and feelings later. We talked on a bit. I can't remember exactly what I said. I assured her of my prayers. Marilyn changed the subject, not abruptly, but somehow we were talking and laughing about Jeremiah. She encouraged us to come back soon, while the leaves were turning. "You didn't get to meet our boys, and we want to meet your children," she said with enthusiasm.

Finally we hung up. I walked to the kitchen table and sat down wiping away a few crumbs. Then I let loose my emotions and cried long and loud. I prayed out loud, too. Even as I prayed I remembered Marilyn's joy and love, her deep concern for others. I remembered how happy she'd been when she went into the villa ahead of us and said, "Here it is, folks!" She'd asked if our food was all right and been concerned about Jeremy. She knew he was sick when we left for Jasper. She had told us of her concern, and of Norm's, for a retreat center at the Chapel and for a place for children with problems to come to. "Somehow, someway, God will provide it," she had said softly. She'd wanted Jerry and me to have a mini-vacation, when she had such needs of her own, and they were never mentioned.

I remembered something she'd told me on the phone right after she told me about the cancer. "I'm not afraid, Marion. I won't live with fear even one day. Each day is too wonderful, a gift."

*She means it. Dear Lord, she means it. It isn't a brave front.*

Whatever other miracles God has in store for Marilyn, she is already living inside one. She has refused the monster of fear that must have tried time and time again to get control of her mind.

Each time I pray for her, I seem to see her—a tiny, fearless creature in the center of those great mountains—looking up—lifting her eyes unto the hills, from whence cometh her help.

# 35

## WHAT I HAVE NEED OF

I was dimly aware that I was trying to go on feelings and there simply were no feelings. I didn't feel Christian or spiritual. God seemed far away. I even felt unloved by Him. I knew better than to go on feelings, but nevertheless that's what I was doing.

It was toward the end of the summer. My daily routine was of waking up to the boys fussing over who got to read the back of the cereal box. In my mind, I knew cereal was spilled under the table and in the chairs. Jennifer wanted to sleep late, and I'd have to get her up and insist that she help me with the housework. She'd been stubborn about it lately. Julie would be at work all day, but I knew before looking that she hadn't left her room in good order.

The kitchen sink continually seemed full of dishes. Someone was always hungry, and everyone fixed his or her own little meal, leaving smeared peanut butter on counter tops and cabinets ajar. Somehow, my family must think that dishes just vanished from the sink. No one bothered to put them in the dishwasher. When they did, they put dirty dishes on top of clean ones.

The bathrooms would be disaster areas unless I kept working constantly at it. I missed the silence of being alone in the house. Someone always needed something, usually at the same time as someone else.

If that wasn't enough, I'd messed up the checkbook again and we didn't have much money. Hardly any. I'd gotten Jon some back-to-school clothes, but they didn't have any in Jeremy's size. With only a week until school started, I was depressed about not having money to buy Jeremy a few things. He could care less. He'd love to go to school with holes in his shoes and pants too short, with the knees out. But he really needed some clothes. It wasn't just a matter of buying back-to-school clothes because September was around the corner.

No big, major problems in my life. Just the same little nagging

ones, but I felt despondent. I could charge him some clothes, I
reasoned. He does need them. But the Lord had been dealing with
me about charging. I'd gotten teaching that overspending and
charging didn't please the Lord. It didn't please Jerry either. If I
hadn't messed up the checkbook, everything would be fine. It had
been another one of my stupid mistakes; I had added instead of
subtracting.

I'd heard glowing testimonies about how the Lord would meet
each need if a person would really put their trust in Him. That
seemed difficult today. Charging seemed simple.

It was Saturday afternoon, and I laid out the boys' clothes for
Sunday school, a habit I had formed to help me on Sunday morning. Julie came in and asked me to drive to a florist with her to get
someone a violet for their birthday. I had a lot to do but figured I
needed a change of scene and so I said yes.

I looked again at Jeremy's pitiful wardrobe and thought: "It
wasn't really a prayer. I suppose the Lord could meet this need, but
I don't even have the energy to ask Him. I'm too tired to pray it
through." I thought about a friend of mine who has fantastic answers to prayers. She simply finds whatever she needs for almost
nothing, or people just give her exactly what she's looking for, or
she actually finds the thing she's praying for on the side of the road
where someone has piled up stuff for the trash man. Once she got
an almost new piece of luggage this way.

I decided God seemed too far away to ask for the clothes for
Jeremy. I couldn't see any way that God could meet my need. "I'm
not even asking," I thought, but in my mind I pictured what I
needed. And I thought, "The Bible says that God knows what we
have need of, and that He's pleased if we have even the faith of a
grain of mustard seed.

"Maybe I have that much faith." I pictured what Jeremy needed.
A pair of shoes, brown. Jeans, brown or tan, and a couple of shirts.
That would be a good start. Way in the back of my mind, I knew
that across the street from the florist there was a store where I
could charge what I needed. But then, the Lord knew what I
needed.

As Julie and Jennifer and I drove toward the florist, we saw a

"Carport Sale Today" sign. We'd been stopping at a few lately since Julie was getting married in a few months. We hadn't found anything she wanted, however.

We pulled in and immediately I saw them. A brand-new pair of shoes, brown. I picked them up to look at the size, but already my faith had grown and I knew they would be a three and a half. They were. They stood out as though glimmering rays came out from them, like a picture in a child's coloring book. I checked the price. Two dollars. In the store, they were eighteen dollars. I walked to a rack of clothes. The first thing I pulled out was a pair of jeans, tan, size 10 (Jeremy's size). Price, one dollar. They appeared to be new. Hanging with the jeans were two shirts that had hardly been worn. Price, fifty cents each. For four dollars I bought exactly what Jeremy needed.

I was so thrilled over my find and that God had had a part in it that I felt bad for a while because my faith had been so small. And I hadn't really wanted to believe that the Lord could meet my need.

Jeremy wore the shoes to Sunday school and church the next day and I saw him sitting in church pulling his pants up a little so his shoes would show. His old ones had been hurting his toes for several weeks. He spit on the shoe and rubbed a small speck of dust off and looked up at me and grinned.

And I, in turn, felt like looking right up at my Father and grinning for His goodness and mercy when I'd been so unbelieving. He knew exactly what I had need of and Jeremy's size. My faith soared, and my prayer life took on new excitement as I sat in church. I asked, now believing and expecting.

What a joy to know that the Lord wasn't angry with me for ever doubting that He could meet my needs. What a God of love!

# 36

## PURRING AND PRAISING

Jerry had taken a Friday off from work and we were eating breakfast at the Waffle House, a couple of miles from our home. It was a rare treat—just the two of us. And I love eating breakfast out. As we got up to leave, I noticed out the window two young men bending down. I couldn't see what they were bending toward, but in my heart I saw.

I *knew* it was a cat! It hadn't been outside when we entered, so someone had probably dumped it while we ate. Maybe the men will take it, I hoped. *Oh, Lord, let them take the cat. Please don't let me have to walk by an abandoned kitten.* I saw the men get into their car. Neither of them held a kitten.

"Jerry," I whispered as we stood at the cash register, "I believe there's a stray cat outside."

A look of agony crossed his face. Not for the cat, but that we had to walk by it. He knew my weakness. I reminded him, "I've been doing pretty good lately. I'm getting where I can walk right by stray cats, even if they look me in the eye."

Jerry sighed and his jaw flinched slightly.

We went outside and there stood the small kitten—skinny, dirty, tired, and quite obviously abandoned. His face and ears had black dirt caked on them. He'd somehow stepped into tar and it had dried on his paws.

As we went outside, the aroma of bacon escaped with us. The red kitten was young and pitifully thin. A few feet away cars whizzed by on the expressway. He wouldn't last long. Nevertheless, I got ready to walk by him—wasn't even going to pet him or say, "Hi, kitty," or go back in and get him a piece of bacon.

But then the foolish cat with everything in the world against him, did the most amazing thing. He rubbed up against my leg and purred, long and loud.

*Purred!* Half-starved, filthy, no hope of getting any of the bacon

from the Waffle House, people ignoring him, and the stupid cat
purred just like he was clean, well fed, and loved.

Without hesitation I stooped and picked him up and held him
close. I could see the fleas on him. He looked right into my eyes
and purred some more. Then he laid his head on my shoulder for a
moment. I could feel his heart pounding. Even in fear, he purred.

If he'd meowed loudly, scampered under a bush, or just sat
silently by the door, I could have walked by him. Jerry and I continued toward the car without speaking. Jerry looked grimly ahead.
I held the purring kitten and smiled foolishly. "I'll try to find him a
home," I said, without looking at my husband.

"Who in the world would take that ugly cat?"

"He has a beautiful face—underneath the dirt."

Jerry had planned to stop by the bank and when he did I got out
and went inside with him. I went to each teller's window and
asked, "Would you like a kitten?" No one even smiled at me. The
cat purred in my arms.

Jerry glared at me from across the bank lobby as if to say, "I'm
not impressed by your attempts."

At home I fed the cat and Jerry asked, "Is it a female?"

"I don't know. Don't think so."

"You never do."

I bathed the cat and fed him some more. Then he hopped into a
little basket I'd placed in the kitchen for him, gave a big sigh, and
went to sleep on his back with his paws crooked slightly up in the
air.

The vet assured me our new kitten was a male, and I promptly
named him Joshua. I'd had this strong wall all built around my
heart that didn't permit any more cats inside. Then Joshua's purring
had made the wall come tumbling down, just like the Biblical
Joshua's marching had caused the walls of Jericho to collapse.

By Joshua's sixth day with us, I'd catch Jerry bending over to pet
him. Sometimes he'd say softly, "Hi, cat. You're looking better."
Joshua picked the foot of our bed to sleep on at night, after he was
certain it was safe. He'd lie very still in order to be able to stay.

I continued to marvel that the cat's purring had resulted in his
finding a good home with all the comforts of life. Finally, I saw a
scriptural parallel one day when I was telling someone that we

should remember to praise the Lord in all situations—even bad ones. I had said, "Anyone can praise the Lord when things are going great, but how it must please and honor God when we make a joyful noise in the midst of gloom and despair."

Right then I wondered if God doesn't feel a little like I had when that desperately hungry and abandoned cat looked up at me and purred, seeming to expect only the best. Why, I'd been overwhelmed. I simply had to respond to his "faith" in me. Everyone knows that starving cats shouldn't purr, they should meow frantically and complain loudly.

Purring and praising seem to be a lot alike, I've decided. Sometimes now when I feel like complaining, giving up, or bellowing noisily, I remember skinny, hungry Joshua and how he purred his heart out that day at the Waffle House. Remembering helps me realize the importance of praising God, especially in bad situations.

It doesn't seem logical that I could see such a powerful truth simply by picking up a stray cat, but then nothing gets my attention as quickly as a stray cat, and the Lord knows that. So like Joshua, who just leaned up against me and purred away, I want to learn to lean against my Father and praise away, regardless of my circumstances.

## AND GILLIGAN TOO

I'd made such a production of our family not watching TV and of the evils of television that I overreacted when one of the boys asked, "Mama, tonight Gilligan and the whole crew get rescued from the island. Let us watch. I mean, let's watch together—please. It's just one hour."

I was all ready to dive into my lecture about zombies that sit in front of a mechanical box while their minds and souls rot away, when Jerry stuck his head in the room. He didn't say anything, but the look on his face spoke clearly to me. *That's a reasonable request, Marion. If you don't say yes, I will.*

"They've been marooned fifteen years, Mama. Let's watch it together."

"Okay," I said grimly, yet, somehow, I felt anticipation about this program. Silly of me, I thought. What could I possibly get from watching Gilligan.

Jon told Jeremy that we were going to watch television together, and that night Jerry, Jennifer, the twins, and I gathered around the set. While Jon turned it on, I reminded everyone of how we used to sit in front of the TV for four or five hours each evening and not communicate with each other and how easy it would be to fall back into that pattern. I elaborated about the filth that now came from most television shows.

"Mama, it's Gilligan," Jeremy reminded me. "There won't be any filth."

I stopped talking when the familiar "Gilligan's Island" music came on. I was astonished to see how much everyone had aged. But then I had too, in fifteen years.

The acting was the same, not too good, slapstick comedy. The lines the characters spoke were practically identical to all their other shows. Lovable Gilligan inevitably goofed things up while desperately trying to help. The props weren't any better than they had ever been. I was highly critical but remained silent. At least the language was decent, if corny.

I hadn't watched television, with a few exceptions, in almost two years, and I was surprised at how annoying the commercials had become. As I sighed and rolled my eyes up in my head to indicate exasperation, Jeremy said, "It'll be over in a minute, Mama."

After it appeared that Gilligan had messed up the entire rescue mission, he and his friends finally escaped from the island. The scene changed and showed the crew being pulled into a harbor in Hawaii. Thousands cheered and threw confetti. All the boats in the harbor came out to welcome Gilligan and his friends. They were aboard their strange-looking houseboat. Dignitaries and nobodies alike welcomed the crew with great enthusiasm and open arms.

All that was being said on the program was soon drowned out by the crowd's cheering. Happy faces cheered the castaways as they neared the shoreline. No words were really necessary.

Right then I did an astonishing thing. My throat suddenly ached and my eyes filled with tears. They ran down my face. There was no stopping them. *What in the world?* I thought. *How can I be crying watching a Gilligan show? No one does that.* Nevertheless, I continued crying and my heart rejoiced triumphantly. I thought for a moment that I might stand up and cheer right there in the den. I looked around at my family without moving my head. None of them was crying. I felt like an idiot.

Then an explanation eased into my mind. The Lord helped me sort it out. *You can learn from this show. I work in many circumstances, even ones you have condemned. You musn't say, "Well, the Lord certainly can't be in that." I have to be in a lot of places to reach all kinds of people. You can learn something here. There's a truth just for you. When one of My lost children is saved, this is how We celebrate in heaven. The angels go wild. They stop everything just to praise and shout and wave their arms. When unlikely people, almost without hope, are rescued, We have a field day, up here. They're home safe, and their names are written in the Lamb's Book for eternity. They've escaped Satan's trap.*

I sat amazed while the old hymn "Rescue the Perishing, Care for the Dying" came to my mind. I wiped away some tears, but more came. I smiled happily. Just then Jon looked my way. "Mama, why are you crying? Do you hate TV that much?"

"No, Jon, I'm crying because . . . because . . ." I didn't think anyone could understand my reasoning and what I thought the Lord had showed me. I knew it sounded foolish to say out loud, even though it seemed so clear to me. Jon waited for my answer. Jeremy looked my way too. Jerry and Jennifer continued to look at the program.

I began, "Well, God has shown me a beautiful truth in this show."

"In Gilligan?" the boys asked at the same time.

"Sure, see how the people are rejoicing? See their genuine joy because the castaways have been rescued. That's how God and all the angels react when someone here gets saved. They look down and say, 'Hey, look-a-there. Old so-and-so is coming into the Kingdom. Hurrah!'"

"Yeah," Jon said, "that's good, Mama, and look at the two bad men they're showing now. They aren't happy. They want to hurt Gilligan. They look like the devil, don't they?"

I nodded joyfully. My boys understood! We might as well have been at a Hallelujah revival.

As soon as the program was over, Jon turned off the television and said, "Thank you, Mama, for watching with us. Can we watch the rest of it next week? There's just one more part."

"Yes, you can." I didn't have to struggle with my answer.

The next day I wondered if I was the only person in the world who'd seen the parallel of a Christian coming into the Kingdom when Gilligan and his friends got saved. At a meeting I was telling someone about my experience while watching the Gilligan show, and someone I didn't know overheard me. She rushed up and commented, "My sister, up north, called and told me that she had almost the exact reaction that you did to that show. She even cried when she saw the salvation message in it."

While working on my Sunday school lesson that I would teach that week, I kept thinking about that television show. Finally, I worked it into my lesson. Maybe no one would understand, but I was going to use it anyway. My children understood, and some woman up north saw what I had seen. When I began telling about the program, many of the girls in the class smiled. They were a new class and it was the first time they had smiled. It made me feel good.

After class one girl didn't leave with the rest of the group. She stayed behind and started crying. Talking was difficult for her. Finally she got it out: "I'm not sure, I mean absolutely sure that I'm saved. I want my name in that Lamb's Book."

The Gilligan illustration had gotten through to her!

She left that classroom, smiling and assured of her salvation. I sat alone in the room for a few minutes. *Oh, Lord, I'm sorry that I so often limit You and try to put You in a box. I always want You to do it my way when You have such neat, unique ways of getting Your message over. Help me be open to expecting Your Presence in unusual places, maybe even places that I don't like or understand.*

# 38

# THEY THAT WAIT

I hate waiting for anything. An agony begins silently inside me, and I want to scream, "Hurry, hurry, can't you?" Often I run up stairs rather than wait for an elevator. Once I left a cart of groceries in a market because I decided the line was too long. No matter which line I choose at the bank or post office, it is inevitably the waiting line. Now the Lord knew my problem, I'm sure, when He matched me up with my husband. Jerry can wait forever for traffic lights to change. When the light turns green I always tell him, "Go, go," fearful that we'll waste a second. He can wait for people to return calls when I'm certain they've lost our number. I guess as a child he waited patiently for Christmas. His patience and ability to wait often infuriate me. He *never* gets in a hurry. He is methodical, and no one can rush him. For twenty years I have waited for him when we are going out. People like Jerry don't understand the frustration that waiting causes people like me.

I believe the Lord is trying to show me how to wait. He's been at it for a long time. I've decided that I might as well try to be teachable because the Lord is one of those patient people, and He's going to keep teaching me. So I'm really trying to learn to wait.

Recently we had a new kitchen floor put down and some carpeting put in the halls and our bedroom. I had selected black carpet for a downstairs bathroom. The carpet man, Mr. Robinson, had assured me that he would have the carpet in within a week or so. He did beautiful work and was very fast. Two years before he'd carpeted our den for us. I knew he was very dependable.

I also knew that I probably wouldn't have to wait with Mr. Robinson doing the work.

Mr. Robinson called to say the company had sent the wrong carpet for the bathroom and there would be a slight delay in finishing that room.

"Okay," I managed. I felt I could deal with that. The wait would probably be just a few days. The second time he phoned, he said they had sent the wrong carpet again.

"Oh," I said weakly, feeling panic trying to come alive in me.

Then I didn't hear from him for a while. When I called he was always out on a job, so I talked with his wife. "Hi, this is Marion West," I'd begin. Finally, I called so much that I was sure when I just said, "Hi," Mrs. Robinson knew who I was. But I explained each time who I was and that I'd been waiting quite a while for my black bathroom carpet. I even told her that I'd thrown the old carpet away when I was redecorating the bathroom and so it was especially hard to wait with the bathroom newly decorated except for the bare floor.

Somehow Mr. Robinson didn't get around to calling me back. About three weeks passed. Julie's wedding date approached. I had to have the carpet before the wedding. I called again, "Hi, this is Marion West." I'd think while I was talking, "Why are you being so nice? Why don't you use an annoyed tone of voice?" But for some reason I'd keep being nice, one more time.

Mrs. Robinson had a lovely telephone voice and assured me that her husband was trying to find the black carpet. When Julie's wedding date was only a few days away, Mr. Robinson came by. I was so happy to see him that I nearly hugged him.

"You're gonna kill me. I know you are. I picked up your carpet—"

I interrupted. "No, I'm so glad you're here. I don't even mind the waiting. You got it!"

He stood with a roll of carpet on his shoulder. "That's the problem. They sent blue." He let me see the carpet. "I've been all over Atlanta trying to find the black carpet. I promised you I could get it."

Two forces battled inside me for control. Anger and peace (the kind that passes all understanding).

"Three days before a wedding is no time to get upset," I reasoned silently. I heard myself say, "It doesn't really matter."

"What!" he said.

"It's okay. I'm not going to get upset about a little piece of carpet. Maybe no one will have to go to the bathroom."

He stared at me silently and asked, "How come you're not pitching a fit?"

I could almost have asked myself that question, but I tried to explain to him and to me. "Well, I have this terrible temper when it comes to waiting. It's a real problem for me. But Jesus has come to live inside me and . . . can you imagine Jesus screaming and hollering and falling apart over a piece of black carpet?"

I almost laughed. He did too. We both seemed relieved. I wasn't going to make a scene.

"I have a temper too," Mr. Robinson confessed. "I'm a Christian and I want Jesus to keep me from losing my temper too. I know it's possible. I just saw you do it. You aren't mad."

"What you are is stupid," a silent voice suggested. "If you'd pitched a fit to start with, you'd have your carpet. You let people take advantage of you."

I stopped listening to the voice. Mr. Robinson said, "I'm gonna get you the black carpet. I promised it to you, but in the meantime how about something temporary? Maybe a dark green?"

"Oh, that would be fine. Could you do that?"

"No problem. I'll be back before the wedding."

He didn't get back.

I waited for a while, then decided to call again. I was having a tea for two friends who were leaving town. I'd like the carpet before the tea. I dialed the familiar number and said, "Hi, this is Marion West."

Mrs. Robinson was extremely polite and said that her husband was coming by with the carpet that very day. "Really," she added, "he'll be there."

I'd waited this long without being rude, so I said with enthusiasm, "Thank you."

"Mrs. West, may I tell you something?"

"Yes, of course." *Please, Lord, let him bring the carpet. I think I'll take purple at this point. No more delays. I've waited so well.*

"Well, I did some work with the youth group at our church and they gave a present. I didn't expect it, but I got a Bible and a book —*Out of My Bondage*. When I saw it was by Marion B. West, I thought, now where have I heard that name? Then I remembered."

We both laughed. How could she ever forget my name? I must have called fifteen times during the past few weeks.

"I like the book so much. I've just started it. I thought how odd that I have the testimony of the woman that my husband is working for. Can't wait to finish it."

After we hung up, I thought, suppose I'd pitched a fit about waiting—even said nice words but with an ugly tone in my voice—my whole testimony would have been a farce to this woman I've never met. *Thank you, Lord, for helping me wait. I know I didn't do it on my own. I'm learning a little bit about waiting.*

Sure enough, Mr. Robinson came that afternoon with a piece of dark green carpet. "Got it," he grinned as soon as I opened the door.

In about fifteen minutes he asked me to come see if it would do until he could get the black. I was amazed at how well it looked to be temporary.

"Oh, it's nice," I exclaimed. "Thank you so much."

We had already discussed that he didn't want me to pay him till he got the black carpet. "I'll be back," he said. "I'll find what you want. Sorry it took so long and that you had to wait."

"It's all right. I need to learn to wait."

He smiled and waved as he drove out of the driveway.

That night all my family peeked in the bathroom and ohhed and ahhed over the carpet. I got the distinct impression that I was missing something the Lord was telling me. Finally I thought I had it. "Jerry, do you think we are supposed to just keep the green carpet and cancel the order for the black?"

"Yes," he said almost before I asked the question. The children agreed.

The next morning I looked at the green carpet one more time. They were right. The green carpet really did something that I hadn't expected. It was beautiful, even though it wasn't the washable kind like I'd wanted. Nevertheless, I felt certain we were supposed to keep it. I called Mrs. Robinson once more and said, "Hi, this is Marion West."

I felt we were friends. She said, "Oh, Marion, I'm reading your book."

I was so used to Mr. Robinson not being home that I didn't even ask to speak to him; I just started telling Mrs. Robinson how much we liked the green carpet.

"Wait, he's here. Talk to him."

Mr. Robinson said, "Hello."

"Oh, hi. I called to tell you that my family loves the green carpet, and I do too, and we don't want the black anymore."

Silence.

I said it another way: "We really love it. I know you're relieved to be finished with this job, and now you don't have to look for the black anymore. Just tell me how much we owe you for this and I'll mail you a check."

"No charge."

"What?"

"No, ma'am. If you like it, I'm glad. Enjoy it. You waited long enough for it."

"Well, thank you, but I'd like to pay you for it."

"No. Absolutely no charge. Just sorry you had to wait."

I hung up the phone beginning to understand that often there is tremendous value in waiting and doing things the Lord's way. Not always yet, but often when I have to wait now, I think, "What's the Lord up to? What's He got in store for me?" Waiting is becoming almost exciting. When I wait I like to claim the scripture, ". . . they that wait upon the Lord shall renew their strength; they shall mount up with wings as eagles; they shall run, and not be weary; and they shall walk, and not faint" (Isaiah 40:31, KJV). Sometimes I even add, "They that wait shall get free carpet for their bathrooms."

# 39

# TRY, TRY, TRY AGAIN

I remember thinking after having my first book published, "I'm so happy writing that if I were put in prison for years, I'd be content if they'd let me have a typewriter and paper." It was a sobering thought. Before writing became a way of life for me, I'd needed people and things to a great extent.

I experienced a period of time in which all I thought about was writing. Everything I saw and did, no matter how humdrum, seemed to be writing material. My mind continually stayed filled with ideas that begged to be put onto paper. I couldn't sleep often, for writing mentally. I'd dream stories, even chapter titles. Sometimes I'd wake up in the middle of the night and look at the clock to see how long it would be before I could get up and write. (My family wouldn't like to hear the typewriter in the middle of the night. During the day was bad enough.)

I slipped into my writing world so deeply that I began shutting out people (including my own family and God). Some days I'd write ten hours a day and be too tired to cook supper. It was exciting after all the years of waiting and hoping, to actually be writing and having publishers accept my work, but it **was** also dangerous. At the rate I was going I'd be all burned out in a year or so. Our family life was suffering. And I felt guilty because I wanted to write all the time.

Finally, an experienced Christian writer gave me some good advice: Get away from it for a while. Only with God's help was I able to do this. But I didn't write for about six months, then when I got back into it my priorities were back into perspective. I was grateful to the Lord for slowing me down. I felt like a runner, a tired runner, who could walk, even sit down sometimes.

During my slowing-down process, I was startled and a little frightened when well-meaning people asked, "When will you start your next book?"

"Oh, I'm never going to write another book—just short articles."

Writing *Out of My Bondage* had been a five-year ordeal that I often ached to quit. It was incredibly hard. I didn't know how to write a book. I always longed to be on the last chapter. At one point when Jerry and I disagreed about something in the book, I allowed myself to become very upset. Jerry had no idea how deeply I had become affected. I kept it all on the inside. I wound up in the hospital with a large ulcer and in a lot of pain. I was very embarrassed because I thought I was too spiritual to have an ulcer. I'd come down off the mountaintop, falling and sliding and scraping myself all the way. In the very bottom of the valley, I thought seriously about not finishing the book. Yet, I knew I had to.

Seemed like there wasn't a happy medium for me. Either I wrote all the time, or just piddled around. Knowledgeable people kept telling me that I'd write a second book, even a third and fourth.

I didn't want to put my insides down on paper again. I didn't want my family to have to tell me that I was letting the house go. I didn't want to wake up in the middle of the night again, writing mentally. And perhaps most of all I felt I couldn't handle the exhaustion that came with writing a book.

The Lord seemed to be telling me, gently, that I was to write a second book. I didn't want to listen. I had a dozen good reasons for not writing a second one. *Lord, let me write articles—short ones—everyday happenings. I can do that and not get so totally involved.* Since I didn't see a handwriting on the wall that said no, I went ahead with my idea. I was greatly relieved not to be writing a book and worked hard, but with joy, on the articles.

As I'd finish each article I had to decide where to send it. Inevitably *Guideposts* seemed to be the place I was to submit the article. I loved working with *Guideposts* editors. Years before, in October 1972, they'd published my first article ("Thank You, Lord, for My Broken Dishwasher"). Since then they'd accepted a few others. In 1976, after having failed on my first entry two years before, I won a trip to the *Guideposts* Writer's Workshop. There were sixteen winners from the United States. That I was one was almost unbelievable. When the mailgram came telling me I'd won, I thought it was junk mail and threw it away. Then, for some reason, I walked back to the trash can, got it out, unfolded it, and read it slowly. It began, "Glad to inform you that you have been selected to attend the *Guideposts* Writer's Workshop in Rye, New York." It was signed, Arthur Gordon, Editorial Director.

I let out a scream that must have been heard for blocks. Then hopped in the car and drove wildly over to show the mailgram to a friend who would understand. She wrote too.

The trip to New York to study with accomplished, inspirational writers was all I'd hoped for—and more. It was harder work than I'd expected, but I loved every minute of it. The only trouble I experienced was that I'd become used to writing under adverse circumstances. Children asking questions, time to start supper, phone ringing, time to pick up a child from cheerleading practice, cat hungry and meowing in my face. At the workshop the silence was profound. I was treated like a queen giving birth. No interruptions. Snacks served quietly on a tray while I wrote. Meals served on time, and I didn't have to do anything but show up. Even then the conversation was about writing. Other workshoppers were happy to critique my work. At home no one in my family wanted to read anything I'd written. At the workshop, all day, each day, no one bellowed, "Mamaaaa . . ."

After I got used to the beautiful silence, I did all right writing.

An editor told us—the workshoppers—that we were now part of the *Guideposts* family. Some writers that I'd admired greatly for years were affiliated with *Guideposts*. *I* was a part of that family. Wow! We were encouraged to send *Guideposts* at least three articles after the workshop. Mentally, I began writing my first one on the plane heading home.

I could just see my article in print. I sent it off jubilantly. The reply came quickly. It was glorious fun hearing from an editor that I knew. The fun was short-lived. My article had been rejected. I knew *Guideposts* could be tricky to write for because certain requirements had to be met in each story. But I'd attended the workshop—learned exactly how to write for them. And had been rejected. Well, I'd try again. Within a week I had another article in the mail to them.

Rejected again.

Tried again.

Rejected.

Weeks of rejections followed. I began putting the rejections in a box. I kept writing articles, and each time one was finished, I'd send it to *Guideposts*. I was supposed to send them something acceptable after the workshop, so I felt an obligation. But I knew that I would have sent the articles to them anyway. I loved writing for them.

Finally there were over twenty-five rejections. Most of the articles were returned with encouraging letters from editors.

I tried again and again.

More rejections.

I couldn't understand it. I became obsessed with getting an article in *Guideposts*. I had to. It became my goal. I'd do it if it took me the rest of my life.

One day after getting another rejection, all my enthusiasm seemed to shrivel up and die. I wanted to quit trying. It was too hard to keep getting rejected. Other workshoppers' stories were appearing in *Guideposts*. Why couldn't I get one accepted? While listening to the radio one evening, I heard the song "I have decided to follow Jesus—no turning back—no turning back." Listening, I began to cry. *Oh, God, I don't want to turn back. But I'm so tempted. I don't have any more energy. Your Son must have been tempted to turn back too—facing all His rejections and the final rejection at Calvary. He didn't turn back. Help me not to turn back either. I can't do it by myself.* For days I sang that song. I'd go to bed thinking about no turning back. I became fascinated with the words and the idea. One night I got out my box of rejections and began thumbing through them. Suddenly I realized that all my articles seemed to have one main theme—*not turning back*. I broke out in gooseflesh.

On top of that box I wrote "No Turning Back." Instantly I knew that I had something in the box besides rejections, and I cried all over the top of the box. *I had a book manuscript.* I'd almost finished a book and didn't even know I'd started one! The Lord had kept the wonderful secret from me. He knew I didn't have the courage to start a second book all along. Now it was almost finished. I tore into the box again, like someone making a wonderful discovery. Carefully I divided the articles into sections. There were six obvious categories of not turning back. I shuffled them out on the floor like I was playing cards. All my stories fell into one of the categories. Then quickly the Lord seemed to give me a special and appropriate scripture to go with each section. It only took a few minutes. It was like having a baby (easily) and not even knowing you were pregnant.

A few months after the book had been released the phone rang one day. The caller said, "Hello, Marion. This is Arthur Gordon at *Guideposts*." He spoke in a warm, friendly voice, and I suddenly felt like one of the *Guideposts* family, even if I'd been rejected over twenty-five times.

I couldn't imagine why he'd be calling me. "I just finished reading your new book. It came across my desk. I like it. Would you be agreeable to our publishing a few chapters as a book excerpt in *Guideposts?* We'll work out the details with your publisher."

I had this overwhelming feeling that I wasn't going to be able to utter a word. Or that if I did, I might just scream into the phone, "Whoopie!"

I swallowed hard and managed in what I hoped was a matter-of-fact voice, "Certainly. Sounds like a good idea." My heart pounded and my face hurt from smiling. *A book excerpt!*

Then he mentioned the chapters that the editors would be choosing the excerpt from.

"But . . . those were turned down as articles. Rejected! I sent them all to *Guideposts* first."

Arthur laughed. "Editors are human," he said. "Sometimes a manuscript looks better the second time around." I had to either laugh or cry, so I laughed with him. It seemed to me that the Lord joined us in the celebration of laughter.

After we hung up I got out the original manuscript of *No Turning Back*—a box of rejects to me—only God had never seen them as that. *Oh, Lord, I'll never understand Your ways. Thank You for not letting me turn back. Thank You for helping me try again and again and again. Help me remember that there are going to be many times when I think I'm in the midst of failure . . . and really it's just part of Your unique plan for me to succeed.*

# 40

# WHO GIVES THIS BRIDE?

Julie's wedding date, December 9, 1978, dawned cloudy. A drizzle fell. The day before had been all blue skies with temperatures in the sixties.

Julie came into my room that morning wearing her old pink robe with the pocket torn almost off. I thought about the elegant gown and negligee her grandmother had bought for Julie's honeymoon. I'd helped her pack it. Her hair was in pink curlers. "How soon do you think the rain will stop?" she asked, looking out the window.

"In time. We won't worry about it."

"Okay," she smiled.

I felt pretty normal—excited, but not really uptight. I'd heard terrible stories about how the mother of the bride got all upset and the wedding day was hectic. The photographer was to be at our house at noon for pictures. The florist would deliver our flowers just before noon. The wedding was set for two. For almost twelve months hundreds of little details had been carefully filed in my mind. One by one they were now taken care of. Everything was going according to our plans and prayers—except for the rain.

A pesky silent voice interrupted my thoughts: "Now you'll fall apart. Julie's really leaving—for good. Your first child, and she's only eighteen. Remember how you did almost fall apart a few months after she'd become engaged? Remember how you cried and hurt, thought you couldn't possibly let her go? Remember?"

I remembered. For months after Julie had become engaged on Christmas Eve, I'd smiled and said all the right things. Then my emotions caught up with me late one Sunday afternoon. I had cried with all my family around watching. I made terrible noises with my throat and cried until I hiccupped. It wasn't an attempt to get Julie to change her mind. I knew her wedding plans and her love for Ricky were as settled as concrete. I loved Ricky and his family too. He was a perfect choice for Julie. It was just that letting go was much more difficult than I'd imagined.

As I had sat on my tall stool in the kitchen crying uncontrollably, all my family had moved away from me one by one. And then one returned to comfort me. Jon. He'd stood by me like a small soldier talking to me simply. But his words were powerful. I knew God was giving him the words to say. Jon had touched my shoulder and spoken positively about the future. He told me that I was going to be all right. Looking at him with ketchup on his mouth and his Keds untied, I knew that somehow the Lord was speaking to me through Jon. I listened to him, as perhaps I've never listened to anyone. My tears stopped. The ache vanished. Joy came to my heart once again as I sat on the kitchen stool with the late afternoon sun coming in through the window. I can't explain it or convince anyone that it happened as simply as it did. But I know that when I cried out to the Lord for help He somehow gave me a healing that day and it lasted.

"Bet your healing is about over," the pesky voice suggested. "Time to fall apart again. Julie's leaving. She'll be in Florida tonight on her honeymoon."

Silently I told the accuser: "The Bible says not to be anxious about anything, but to pray about everything. The Bible says that marriage is of God. The Bible says that the Holy Spirit will never leave me comfortless. God's Word says I can do all things through Christ Who strengthens me. His Word also says . . ."

The accuser fled.

We were all dressed—even the boys. They looked handsome in their brown tuxes. So did Jerry. I kept staring at him. Then I peeked in the mirror and decided I didn't look so bad either. "Hey, Julie, we look sort of like the families in the brides' magazines you've been reading."

She came into my room. "Yeah, I was just thinking that. I love your dress."

We were careful not to say anything that might trigger tears or deep emotions.

The flowers arrived on time—and I praised the Lord silently. I love promptness. The photographer arrived on the appointed dot, and others in the wedding party drove up for pictures. As I looked out the window, I exclaimed, "Julie, it's stopped raining!"

She came to see, and we marveled together.

The picture-taking went well. The boys were really behaving. Then it was time to get in the car and go to the church.

"What about when she walks down the aisle?" The deceiver tried again to upset me. I remembered at rehearsal, when Julie and Jerry had started down the aisle as the music swelled, my face had crumbled for a moment and I had shed unexpected tears. So had my mother. But then we both smiled quickly and I was all right again.

I had anticipated that this might be the moment to get emotional, and Julie had asked me please not to cry, so I'd asked Jo Ann, my dear friend and our church organist to play "Learning to Lean" just before the wedding march. She agreed and loved the idea. She also would play Bill Gaither praise hymns, including "Alleluia." I knew that music would help me, and Julie liked the idea too.

At the church we waited until the director, Julie's and Ricky's Sunday school teacher, called for us. We sat in little nursery chairs, because we were waiting in the kindergarten area. I remembered when Julie used to fit in little chairs like these and her feet didn't even touch the floor. What a short time ago it had been.

She wasn't a bit nervous. I was grateful. Everyone seemed calm and everything was going smoothly.

Finally it was time for Jeremy to usher me to my seat. I got my first glimpse of the church and the people. I was grateful that so many of our friends had come. *Thank You, Father, for these people.* The candles flickered and glowed and I walked down the aisle holding on to Jeremy's arm—even though I knew perfectly well that I was in reality leaning on the arm of Jesus.

In just a few moments, after the three attendants had come in, the music told me it was time for Julie and Jerry to enter. I stood and looked back. Julie and Jerry stood in the door. Julie's happiness seemed to light up the aisle as they came forward. Jerry smiled. I was smiling too. No tears were inside me. *Thank You, Lord. Praise Your name.*

I smiled throughout the ceremony. I had brought along a Kleenex, however. Seemed like the Lord had reminded me to. I heard a strange noise and looked over. Jerry had taken his place beside me and had begun to cry. I slipped him the Kleenex, remembering that it had been Jerry who had cried when Julie was saved at the age of nine. Jerry, who insists that he is not emotional whatsoever, took the Kleenex, looking straight ahead. I also noticed Jon wiping away a quick tear, standing erect. He and Jeremy stood at their designated places in the wedding party like soldiers at Buckingham Palace. They didn't exchange one cross word. *Thank You, Lord.*

When the minister had asked, "Who gives this bride?" Jerry had replied loudly, "Her mother and I do." And I had prayed silently, *With Your help, Lord, not on my own.*

I'd been completely surprised as Jerry and Julie had come down the aisle. They stopped by me. "What's happening?" I'd thought. "Isn't he going to give her away?" This hadn't been in rehearsal. I felt a moment of near panic. Then Julie leaned over and kissed me. Her veil fell across her face and mine, so that for a moment we were both inside it. It was our special moment. "I love you," she whispered, handing me a white rosebud. I held her for a brief moment, rejoicing that the Lord had given me the desire of my heart. I had thought so much about how when Julie came down the aisle she'd be so close to me, yet so far away: I couldn't touch her or speak to her. I didn't tell anyone about these thoughts.

As Julie and her daddy had proceeded on to meet the minister, I smiled even more and held on to my rose like the Statue of Liberty holds her torch—only I didn't hold it over my head.

All through the ceremony I rejoiced. Julie was in the Lord's perfect will for her life. I knew that now. The ceremony was almost over. The vocalist sang "My Tribute" (To God Be the Glory) while Julie and Ricky knelt. I could have shed a few tears then—tears of joy—but I didn't. The minister announced, "May I present to you Mr. and Mrs. Richard Garmon."

The music swelled again and they left joyfully, hurrying up the aisle. Jon came to escort me. I smiled all the way up the aisle. At the reception I kept smiling and had fun. I kept marveling that everything was taking place exactly as we'd planned it. No slipups or goofs. No sadness!

It was all over quickly, and they were gone. Julie forgot one small bag, and suddenly we were chasing them to give it to them. Both our cars stopped in the middle of the street. Traffic halted both ways. I jumped out of our car before it stopped completely,

holding the top of a wedding cake and my white rose in one hand
and Julie's forgotten bag in the other. She rolled down the window,
and I handed it to her quickly. Julie smiled. I smiled back. People
watching from their cars smiled, and I felt that the Lord smiled
down from heaven and said, "See, you didn't have to be sad. I
healed you of sadness that Sunday when you were sitting on your
kitchen stool."

Back at home after our families had left, the enemy said once
again, "Now the letdown will come." Other mothers of brides had
told me how tired and sad they were suddenly when it was all
over. Some had even gone to bed for days or were reduced to tears.
"It's a good time for a virus to hit," someone had told me, "you're
so worn out."

I didn't feel weak or tired. Actually I felt elated, almost like I'd
just gotten married. I was fascinated with Jerry in his tux. I kept
following him around and looking at him. "Let's go out and eat," I
suggested.

"Aren't you tired?" he asked, surprised. I don't have a lot of energy and often tire easily, especially when I have to stand up for a
long time.

"Not a bit."

"Fine, let's go," Jerry said. Jennifer offered to keep the boys for
us. I begged Jerry to wear his tux but he refused—nicely. "Tell you
what, I'll buy one and sit around the house in it and you can just
look at me."

After we were home and in bed and I was still smiling in the
darkness, the phone rang. I answered on the first ring. Julie said,
"Hey, Mama, I wanted you to know that we're in Valdosta at the
Ramada Inn. Our room is pretty. We just ate at the Pizza Hut and
we're drinking Sprite. We'll go on to Disney World tomorrow. Just
wanted you to know we got here okay. Bye."

"Good-bye, Julie," I answered.

I went to sleep smiling. The next morning when I awakened, the
enemy was waiting: "Bet you're tired. Don't feel like teaching Sunday school."

"The Lord is my strength," I told him. I taught, still not tired or
sad. Before we left for Sunday school I walked into Julie's pink and
white room and looked around. The enemy had told me that I

couldn't do that without crying. I sat on her bed and felt only joy for her new life, and for God's miracle in my life: I'd let her go!

Thursday night they came in from their honeymoon to bring us oranges. I was sitting on the steps in the hall looking out the window thinking: "They just might come by here when they get in. They just might."

Suddenly they were driving up our driveway. They got out of the car and hurried inside. It was cold. They didn't even have on coats. They were smiling and looking so happy, so in love.

The enemy even told me that Julie wouldn't be able to handle school, working, and making a home, too. But she assumed her housekeeping tasks with enthusiasm. Cooking breakfast was a labor of love for her (I still don't like to do it). She cleaned their little home thoroughly, delighted in trying out new recipes, and continued working for the two vets. A week and a half after the wedding, she'd written all her thank-you notes. When her grades came in from college to us, she'd made all A's.

On Christmas Eve our family was invited over to her home to see their tree. When we entered, the lights were out, only the lights from the tree shone. A small nativity sat on the coffee table. "Silent Night" was coming from the record player. The house was spotless. Julie served warm, homemade cookies, and Ricky sat on the sofa and adored her without realizing his love showed so openly.

No one spoke. We sat and looked at the large tree and listened to the music and felt the beautiful feelings that were in that house. Even the boys were quiet. It was a silent moment of worship.

Later, I commented to Jennifer that the minute we went into their home I felt something special—happiness, warmth, love—the Lord's presence. It was all there from the moment we stepped in the door.

"Me too," Jennifer said. "I thought it was just me feeling it. I think it's the kind of home they have." I nodded, remembering the plaque they'd bought for the den. It said that Christ was the head of their home.

So when people ask me almost cautiously, "Do you miss Julie terribly?" I'm confused about how to answer. To say no, sounds unnatural. But somehow, someway, I don't. Not the aching kind of missing someone. The accuser failed to inflict any depression on me. He failed completely! And God has given me such happiness for Julie and Ricky that I could easily do cartwheels in the front yard.

But not for one moment do I think that I was able to let go of her and experience this joy from any strength of my own.

Jerry and I gave Julie away through the magnificent power of a loving and understanding God. Who could understand letting go of a child any better than a God who gave away His only child?

# 41

## LAURIE'S GIFT

The unfamiliar voice on the other end of the phone said, almost apologetically, "Hi, you don't know me, but I just finished reading your book—*Out of My Bondage*—and, well, I haven't thought about anything like that—God—in a long time. I don't usually read books about religion. I was wondering if I could come by and talk to you a few minutes. I mean, if you're not busy. I don't usually do things like this. So if you don't have time, it's all right."

I had an appointment in less than two hours and a dirty house, but the fact that this caller was so willing *not* to come, made me want to meet her right then. I encouraged her to come by.

"I can be there in twenty minutes," she said and hung up.

When I answered the door, I realized that Laurie Walker's* telephone voice matched her looks. Friendly and easy to meet. She was smiling. I invited her in and she explained, "I'm on my lunch hour." We sat at the kitchen table and I made coffee. Even then, I thought, she isn't going to just breeze into my life and then out again. This will be a lasting relationship. Laurie told me about her job selling advertisements for a newspaper. She seemed very efficient. Her large brown eyes made conversation easy. She was a good listener. I talked a little about myself and family.

"I just got your book the other day. Funny, the way I found it." Laurie brushed her medium-length reddish brown hair back from her face. "I was waiting to call on a customer in a shopping center and it was so cold. Almost nothing was open except a Christian bookstore, so I went in to get warm. I felt out of place right away. All those books about God and soft music playing—people singing about the joy of the Lord. I was so self-conscious that I went to the children's section to get something for my girls. I didn't need God, you know, but my children did."

* Real name not used.

I nodded. I liked Laurie. She wasn't going to pull any punches. Her honesty was refreshing.

She continued, "When I started back, there was a copy of your book on the counter. It jumped out at me with all those hundreds of books in the store. I just stood there and looked at it and thought about the title—*Out of My Bondage*. I finally admitted to myself that I was living in bondage of a terrible kind. I tried to walk on but couldn't. I just kept staring at the book. I looked in my purse and didn't have enough money to buy it. I forgot about the children's books and asked the clerk if he would save it for me. He said he would. Well, when I got home I tried to forget about that stupid book. I really did. Saturday morning, we woke up and it was raining—bucketsful. My girls were fussing. I have two little girls. I'm divorced. All I thought about was getting dressed and dragging the girls out in that rain to get the book. Ridiculous. I don't even read religious books.

"But we went. I got the book and came home and read it straight through. I started thinking about God again. I knew Him as a child. I've strayed so far away."

Laurie wasn't smiling now. Her eyes brimmed with tears. She glanced at the clock and speeded up her story. "I've been living with a guy, but he moved out a few weeks ago. I still see him. Some of his stuff is at my apartment. He still has a key to the apartment. I'm wild about him." She hesitated for a moment, then continued, "You have all this." She threw her arms up for a moment, indicating a secure home in the suburbs, a husband . . . the normal Christian life. "I live on the other side. I see things you wouldn't believe. I do things you probably wouldn't believe." She laughed nervously.

I looked her straight in the eye and kept listening. I liked Laurie even more. She was genuine.

"I've been on drugs. I'm not getting any child support from my ex-husband. I scream at my children. I'm tired. Nothing makes much sense."

She was silent for a moment and I was too. Softly she asked, without even looking up, "Do you think my life could ever be . . . straightened out?"

She looked at me as she finished the question, brushing her hair back from her face. I nodded, "Won't be easy."

"Nothing has ever been easy for me."

She seemed to be waiting for me to say something, so I said, "You have to start somewhere. Do you think you could take your boyfriend's things back to him? Get your apartment key back?"

Tears filled her eyes. "I could try."

We talked on for a while longer about how Jesus changes a person from the inside out—makes all things new.

"I'd like to be new," Laurie sighed, "but I'm so weak."

"That's who He helps," I said excitedly. "He can't help strong people. You're a perfect candidate!"

Laurie left, and later in the week we met for lunch. She appeared calm and self-secure, dressed in a smart three-piece tailored suit. While we ate, she told me, "I'm going to start going to church somewhere." Laurie had told me that as a child she'd asked Jesus into her heart and now she wanted forgiveness—wanted to get back in touch with Him. She said most of all she wanted peace.

Later in the week she called and said she had returned all Phil's* (her boyfriend's) things. He gave her her key back. She sounded excited and happy.

A few days later, when Laurie and I were talking, she said she'd like to visit my church. She didn't want to go by herself, so she drove with her little girls over to my house and picked me up. The rest of my family came on in our car. In her car, I met her children, Kim and Kathy,† for the first time. Laurie seemed nervous about going to church. "Everything in the world has gone wrong." Her voice was high and tense. "I overslept, burnt the toast, couldn't find Kathy's good shoes." Kathy looked up at me and smiled and showed me her old shoes.

"Sunday is the devil's favorite day for making church people late," I laughed. "Welcome to the club."

At our church, I took my new friends to their classes. I'd told Laurie's teacher, Dawn Johnson, a little about Laurie and that I'd be bringing her to class. Dawn was waiting at the door and she said

* Real name not used.
† Real names not used.

even before I could introduce them, "Oh, you must be Laurie. Welcome." Then she hugged her. When they separated, Laurie looked relaxed.

Things seemed to be going well for Laurie and her little girls. We talked on the phone occasionally. She attended my church some, but mostly she worshiped at another, larger church near her apartment. Nine-year-old Kim accepted Jesus, and Laurie made a recommitment to Him. Kim was baptized, and they became members of the church. I got little gold crosses for both Laurie's girls, and she said they loved them. They talked about Jesus openly in their home. Laurie began reading the Bible and Christian books. She was a fast reader and often read two a day. She and Dawn became close friends, and Dawn taught her a lot about how to live the Christian life on a day-to-day basis.

Phil, even though he'd moved out of Laurie's apartment, began to question her about God. He saw the changes in her life and wanted to know more. She agreed to see him to tell him about Jesus and what He meant to her now. She didn't push her beliefs on Phil, but only answered his questions as best she could. Laurie hadn't felt that she'd done a very good job of explaining how Jesus enters a life to Phil. He was a middle-aged, partying bachelor who'd never thought about God before. However, Phil began attending the same church Laurie had joined. He went forward for salvation one day and was baptized that evening and started attending regularly.

I was having an autograph party for my second book at the bookstore where Laurie had bought a copy of *Out of My Bondage*. I looked up and there she stood with tears streaming down her face. Her hands trembled. She appeared ready to collapse.

"What's the matter, Laurie?" I whispered and hugged her. No other people were around just then.

She closed her eyes and new tears squeezed out. "Help me. Please help me. I'm not going to make it. Nothing is going right. Phil came back last night, and I let him in just to talk for a few minutes."

She dropped her head and cried.

Hesitantly I asked, "How long did he stay?"

She struggled with her answer. "Long enough," she said softly.
"I'd be better off dead. I really would."

"Let me call Dawn and if she's at home, will you go see her? I
have to stay here and can't talk now."

She nodded. Dawn was at home and wanted Laurie to come
over. She and Dawn talked a long time. Dawn set up more appointments for counseling for Laurie with her and her husband, Charles,
who is a minister. Laurie kept the appointments. She seemed to be
on the right road again. She and her girls attended church faithfully, even though she didn't like having to see Phil there. He also
attended regularly.

A few weeks later, Laurie called. I was glad to hear from her.
Our last conversation had been bright. Laurie said in a serious
voice: "Marion, I have something to tell you and you may not want
to see me again. I'm pregnant. It's confirmed. Can I come to talk
with you, and will you call Dawn and see if she'll come too? If you
don't want to see me, it's okay."

"Laurie, of course I want to see you. I'll call Dawn and call you
right back."

Dawn could come the next morning, so I phoned Laurie right
back and told her to come around ten.

Dawn and I were already sitting at my kitchen table when the
doorbell rang. I let Laurie in and Dawn jumped up and we were all
three hugging each other. Laurie tried to joke, even though there
were tears in her eyes. "I knew it! You two would hug me no matter
what. How can you love me?"

We sat back down and Laurie said, "Well, I have several
choices." She named them. "Abortion, raise the baby alone, get Phil
to marry me, or give it up for adoption."

Dawn said quickly but softly, "As a Christian, abortion is out. It's
murder, Laurie."

Laurie cried openly and said, "I know it. But I always planned to
have an abortion if I ever got pregnant. Now I can't. Phil wants me
to."

I was shocked. We knew Phil said he was now a Christian. Even
if he was a baby Christian, he must know that abortion wasn't an
answer.

After two hours of conversation, the three of us held hands sitting at my kitchen table and claimed that baby for the Lord. Laurie's tears fell onto the table, and she about squeezed my hand in two. Dawn added, "Whether you keep it or give it away is up to you, but those are your choices—your *only* choices."

"How will I know what to do?" Laurie cried.

"You ask the Lord. He will direct you. He knows best. If He tells you to keep it, then do it. He'll give you the strength and the peace. If He tells you to give it up, He'll give you the strength and peace for that too. We can't tell you what choice to make, but we'll stand by you. Listen to the Lord and lean heavily on Him."

Later Laurie told us that she hoped Phil would marry her. He'd stopped begging her to have the abortion, but he complained that she'd ruined his social life. He was depressed and couldn't sleep. Finally he told Laurie to get out of his life—not to speak to him when they met. He also told her about the new girls he was dating. And each Sunday she saw him in Sunday school.

Laurie told me that she was trying to depend totally on Jesus in order not to be bitter toward Phil. But bitterness was creeping in. Phil didn't want to help her financially. "He just wants to wash his hands of the whole thing," Laurie said. In the meantime, her ex-husband came back through town and came to see her. When he learned of the situation, he tried to get her to have an abortion. Laurie's mother told her that she would disown her because of what had happened. Her sister was heavily involved with hard drugs—taking them and selling them. She couldn't help Laurie.

Laurie was learning to lean on Jesus. There wasn't anyone else.

People where she worked asked openly, "Why don't you have an abortion?" One man told her, "My wife has had four. We don't want any children. There's nothing to it. Everybody's doing it."

When Laurie went to be certain she was pregnant, she had the test made at an abortion clinic. She told me, "It was lovely—the office. Thick carpet, expensive furniture, stereo music, smiling efficient people moving about quietly. Good magazines to read. The receptionist told me that she got her job through having an abortion there. She said there was nothing to it." Laurie said, with difficulty, "All those people there were waiting to kill a baby. In the back were murdered babies. Do you know it hurts them? They can feel. Even at twelve weeks, they look just like a baby—only very small. All the carpet and stereo in the world doesn't make it right. Neither does the fact that the law says it's all right. The Bible says God knew us in our mother's womb ("Before I formed thee in the belly I knew thee." Jeremiah 1:5, KJV) and John the Baptist was filled with the Holy Spirit from his mother's womb. This baby is going to live," Laurie said with determination.

Laurie had another reason to lean on Jesus. Her Sunday school teacher, when he learned of her situation, advised her to get legal help. There was a lawyer in her church, and Laurie went to talk with him. She told me that she really thought he'd pray with her and give her scriptures, but instead he wanted to take her case. He said they could make Phil pay. Laurie had timidly mentioned to the lawyer about trusting in the Lord and he had replied that we "have to handle some things ourselves."

So she told the lawyer to go ahead with the case and he wrote Phil a letter. But Laurie hadn't slept well after her decision to sue, and she phoned Dawn to tell her what she'd done and that she didn't feel good about it.

Dawn quickly told about the scripture that teaches that Christians don't sue Christians. Laurie read the scripture for herself from The Living Bible in I Corinthians 6:1–8 and she agreed with God's Word.

She had asked Dawn, "But what can I do now?"

Dawn had explained there was only one thing to do, "Call Phil and apologize. Ask him to forgive you for even considering suing and drop the suit."

Laurie had screamed, "I can't. I can't apologize to *him!*" But even as she said the words, she knew that she would—somehow. She had to have peace at any cost.

She phoned Phil and said matter-of-factly that she was sorry and asked his forgiveness.

He accepted her apology. Laurie then phoned the lawyer and told him to drop the suit.

A few months before the baby was due, Dawn somehow crossed the path of a minister who sometimes helped arrange adoptions. Dawn took his name and number in case Laurie chose this route. Then as time for the birth drew nearer the Lord spoke to Laurie and told her to give up the baby. He instructed her to let Dawn make the arrangements with the minister, who knew of a Christian couple who had prayed for years for a baby.

Laurie told Dawn and me, "I'm growing this baby for someone else. I don't understand how I'll give it up, but the Lord will help me. He's working out all the details. God will work something beautiful out of my ugly mistake."

"What about your girls?" I had asked.

"I told them that I loved them so much and I was so grateful to have them. Then I explained that some people can't have a baby—ever. 'Girls, we have each other. What do you think about our giving this baby to someone who will never have one, unless someone is willing to share?'

"The girls thought for a few minutes and decided that sharing was a good idea.

"As soon as I made the decision, the Lord gave me such a peace that I knew for sure I'd made the right decision. I'd never known such peace in my life. I knew it wouldn't be easy, but I know that with God anything is possible. He's worked out so many miracles in my life. My mother and I have a good relationship now. She's forgiven me. My sister has become a Christian. I have no bitterness toward Phil. I pray for him daily. I don't want him to feel guilty. I want him to experience the full love of God. The girls and I have started praying for their daddy. He's out of the States, but we're asking the Lord to bring him back. Maybe, just maybe, someday we can be a family again. I'm willing and the girls want their daddy back. The Lord is allowing me to tell my girlfriends, girls who are still living like I was, about Jesus, and how He makes all things brand-new."

Laurie told me that she'd had trouble carrying her girls full term. In fact, her first baby had been born almost three months early. There were problems with carrying her second child to full term. She explained, "The Lord's keeping this baby till it's ready to be born. I just know it won't be early."

There were complications during the pregnancy. Laurie gained a lot of weight and she had Rh-negative blood. She needed special treatment that was costly. A Christian friend of mine managed a health department, and she took a personal interest in Laurie. Laurie qualified for a program that allowed her to receive medical treatment, plus food. Laurie had been praying about each of her needs as they arose. Food became a very real need. On the program at the health department, milk and other food was delivered to Laurie's front door. One reason for the financial problems was that she had been fired at work. She took that problem to the Lord too, and her needs continued to be met. The Lord gave her the scripture in Proverbs 10:3: "The Lord will not suffer the soul of the righteous to famish . . ." (KJV). Also a comfort to her was Psalms 37:25: ". . . nor have I seen the children of the godly go hungry" (TLB).

Laurie remained keenly aware of the needs of others in her own need. The Lord impressed me to give her a certain amount of money. I wasn't sure how to go about it. I didn't want it to be awkward. She received it warmly, so that I felt good about it. Later she told me that she gave a fourth of it away. "I met someone with a *real* need," she had said.

I heard Laurie's testimony several times. She told it painfully and honestly. That she was a new creation was obvious. Her face glowed with love for the Lord and for other people as she spoke. Her main theme seemed to be forgiveness. "I can't be angry with Phil, or blame him," she'd say. "The Lord has healed me of bitterness. I can pray for Phil. How can anyone refuse to forgive?" Laurie would ask with tears streaming down her face. "From the agony of the cross Jesus asked, 'Father, forgive them.' Don't let bitterness stay in your heart," she'd urge others. She also made her feelings about abortion quite clear. "I could no more kill the baby inside me than I could go home and shoot my two little girls."

Laurie's baby was overdue, and her doctor decided to induce labor. I went to the hospital with her, and Dawn kept one of her children. Her mother kept the other one. I sat back in the labor room with her for six hours. However, the pains would not get hard enough. We talked, laughed, or just sat quietly looking at each other. Her spirits were good.

"Don't you know they're excited," she said at one point.

"Who?"

"The baby's parents. They've waited for so long. I guess they've got all the things you buy for a baby. I've been thinking about that. I want the baby to have everything he needs."

"Oh, I'm sure they have enough for three babies," I said. "They must be so grateful to you and the Lord."

After six hours Laurie was dismissed from the hospital in bitter disappointment.

Almost a week later Dawn got a call from the hospital. We were at church. They'd induced labor again, and Laurie had given birth quickly—to a boy, over eight pounds. She and the baby were both fine.

"So," I thought, "he's finally here—this much-prayed-for and wanted child." I went to see Laurie the next morning. She'd been moved off the O.B. floor and was in a private room. She looked tired, still swollen, but obviously happy. "I'm fine—just fine. The baby is too. Don't you know his parents are excited. They know he's here. They tried to knock me out in the delivery room. Gave me enough to knock out a horse, but I stayed wide awake. I saw him come into the world—saw my stomach go flat and empty." She also told me that she was considering going to the nursery to see him once. I didn't comment. She smiled, "The Lord will tell me exactly what to do."

Later I learned that she had seen the baby. Dawn had been with her. "I knew the minister and his wife were coming to get the baby and that if I didn't see him then, I never could. I walked to the nursery leaning on Dawn. She really held on to me. I felt like . . . Jesus was walking with us, too. I couldn't have looked at the baby with my own strength. When we got there, the nurse turned him around facing us. Dawn and I just stood there crying and laughing and holding on to each other. And then the Lord gave me the strength and peace to turn around and walk away. I don't know how it was possible. There wasn't room for sadness. I can't explain it. My peace was tremendous."

Laurie also told me, "I'd had some counseling about giving up the baby. The lady told me that I must expect to grieve like it had died when I gave him up. She told me to expect to suffer terribly. I was terrified of grief. I have grieved over so much in my life. Especially giving up Phil. I didn't want more grief. And it didn't come!

The peace that passeth all understanding came instead. Isn't the
Lord wonderful! I knew I could never give up my baby—but God
showed me how. He did something else, too. He gave me an even
greater love for my children. I'm a new kind of mother. And in return I gave the children back to the Lord. At first I just gave Him
little things. My apartment, my clothes, my car . . . but then I had
to give Him everything. He's in complete charge now. Just think,
the woman at the well was in good shape compared to me . . . and
God has made me brand-new. I wanted to die I was so miserable
with my sins. They're all gone. He took them all."

I was glad we were talking on the phone because I started crying, but didn't sniff or anything. I just wiped the tears away quietly
and kept my voice normal.

She continued, "I have been thinking about how the baby's parents had waited so long for him. Waited and prayed. Then they had
to wait all that day, the day they got him. Don't you imagine they
stood at the window and watched cars coming down the street . . .
and finally a car turned in their driveway, and at last, they had
their son! I keep thinking about that."

Laurie went home from the hospital the day after the baby did.
She had a problem with bleeding and bled for nine weeks. Finally
the doctor said she'd have to have a D and C. Laurie explained to
me that she didn't have any insurance and had panicked. Then the
Lord spoke to her and said, "Laurie, I will meet all your needs if
you'll let Me." That very night when she asked Him to heal her, the
bleeding stopped instantly.

And even while I was working on this chapter Laurie called and
said, "He's still doing it, Marion, working miracles in my life. My
ex-husband has come back to the States and has been in touch with
us. God brought him all the way across an ocean. I'm ready to try
again when he is. In the meantime the girls and I pray for him each
morning and each evening. I can't wait to see what the Lord will
do with him as soon as my ex-husband is ready. Each day there's
some new miracle in my life. Jesus meets all my needs. He's even
found me a new job—I start Monday."

Laurie almost never mentions what she gave up—a son. All she
ever raves about is what God's Son gave her—new life—and, at
last, peace.

## LEANING TOGETHER

For almost a year I'd been bombarding heaven with complaints about the fact that Jerry and I didn't get to spend much time together. I figured that some days we saw each other only about eight minutes. But, even then, he was often preoccupied with business or a ballgame on television, or a child stood at his side, asking for help with math.

The problem grew to enormous proportions as far as I was concerned. I tried again and again to explain to Jerry what I was experiencing and that we must spend time together. He agreed, but we couldn't seem to squeeze it in.

The problem was mine. Jerry didn't seem to have a need to sit for hours at a time alone with me, or make small talk. If it worked out so that we could, that was fine with him, but he wasn't panicky about it, like I was becoming.

It had gotten so I resented the children rushing to him first when he came home from work. He always seemed to have time to listen to them talk about something like a tree fort or a ball score. "That's being a good father," I told myself. "Surely I can't resent that." But truthfully, deep inside, I did. I even resented the children coming into our room so often. They'd pop in, sit on the dresser, bed, or floor and start talking—usually to their daddy. Jon, especially, followed him like a shadow. "Some people can't communicate with their children," I reasoned. "I should be grateful for this. Some mother you are."

Perhaps, most of all, I wanted Jerry to sit in the kitchen with me while I did the dishes and just watch me or talk—about anything. I'd even talk about football! He did it sometimes because I begged him to so much, but I never felt he really needed to stay and talk with me.

I told a friend that if the Lord didn't work it out so that Jerry and I could spend more time alone together, I felt like I'd burst. I thought about it hours each day and even when I got into bed at night. I go to bed early and Jerry is a night owl, so I often felt resentment during the night.

Saying my same need over and over sounded like nagging, so I tried to keep quiet about it, hoping for a miracle. I cried about it. Prayed. Read the Bible. Mumbled, and determined to do better.

The problem got worse.

I became almost a fanatic about Jerry needing me in small ways. I felt convinced that he didn't need me the way I wanted him to.

One of Jerry's "hobbies" is taking long, soaking baths with the tub filled to the brim. Maybe he reads in there or makes important decisions or sleeps. I don't know, but he sometimes takes two such baths a day. I can take a bath in three minutes. I start bathing while the water is still running in the tub and can be finished when there's four inches of water. Jerry won't even get in till the tub's full.

I even started resenting his taking a bath!

I knew fully that my feelings were unreasonable, so I felt guilty on top of feeling not needed.

One Saturday Jerry decided to trim limbs from trees in the back yard. Jon was at his side helping. I watched from the kitchen window, feeling even more separated from Jerry. I decided to work on this book. When I wrote, I seemed to forget about any problems. So I was happily typing when the back door opened, and I knew by the way Jerry slammed it that he was angry. He came down into the den, with Jon close by. Somehow, he wasn't walking normally. I couldn't figure out what was the matter. He sat on the sofa and I stopped typing and asked, "What's the matter?"

"I did a stupid thing. Fell. I've done something to a muscle in my arm."

He supported his right arm with his other one.

"How high did you fall from?"

"About five feet. Landed on my shoulder. The ladder just went out from under me, like it was knocked."

"Can you lift your arm?"

"No," he said quickly. "Must be a muscle spasm."

Jerry looked grimly at the arm and made a decision. "You've got to take me to the emergency room."

I was surprised. Jerry doesn't seek medical help much. For one thing, he's almost never sick—or hurt.

I knew at the emergency room there could be a five-hour wait for X-rays, so I phoned Julie and Ricky to have them check on Jen and the boys. Ricky answered and wanted to take Jerry. I agreed and continued with my typing.

In a couple of hours Ricky called. He and Julie had plans for the evening and he was coming home. Jerry wanted me to come on up in an hour or so. He thought he'd be ready to come home by then.

When I got to the emergency room, Jerry sat reading. It had been over four hours and he hadn't had any treatment. He still held his arm. I'd brought Jon with me because he'd begged to come and I knew he'd be content no matter how long we had to wait, just so he could be near his daddy.

Finally, X-rays were taken and read. The large bone in Jerry's upper arm was broken in two, about three inches below the shoulder. The doctor explained that it was a very bad break.

We were stunned. He hadn't complained much with pain. The arm was set quickly. Jerry didn't have any medication, until after it was set, but he said it didn't hurt much. With his arm in a cast and in a sling that kept the arm strapped to his body, we were ready to go. An orderly rolled Jerry to the exit in a wheelchair. Jon walked along with his daddy, and I ran to get the car.

Before we left, Jerry mentioned something to me about going to work in a car pool and that he wouldn't have to drive. The doctor overheard and was at our side instantly. He was Spanish and spoke in short, imperative sentences without wasting words: "No work until I say. Do almost nothing. Sit up while sleeping. Get a hospital bed if you like. No baths. I'll see you Tuesday." He'd turned to me and in a softer voice said, "He'll be okay. Don't think we'll operate. Take care of him." Then he patted my shoulder.

I felt like screaming, "No bath! Man, you don't know what you're saying." But I nodded efficiently and said, "Yes, sir."

We drove home in silence, still stunned. Jon often looked at his daddy's arm and his shirt draped over him but didn't comment.

Jerry had trouble getting comfortable sitting up in bed, and the next day, even though it was Sunday, I was able to locate a hospital bed. A friend of ours went with me to get it in his truck. When we got it set up in our bedroom, Jerry eyed it suspiciously.

Sunday night, he decided to get in the tub. "I'll only sit in a couple of inches of water." He got in without difficulty, but getting out proved to be somewhat of a problem. He flinched once, like he'd moved his arm.

When we went back to the doctor on Tuesday, the bone had slipped a little and the arm had to be reset. Jerry didn't mention getting in the tub again.

The cast didn't bother Jerry as much as the sling which kept his arm strapped to his body. His hand had begun to swell. His mobility was greatly limited. He'd never depended on me for things, and suddenly he had to lean on me for the simplest of things. In fact, I saw that we were going to have to learn to work together. From our previous experiences at hanging wallpaper, I knew we had problems ahead.

I'd ask him early in the morning, "Do you need anything?"

At first he just stared ahead, not answering me. With three children to get off to school, I couldn't wait indefinitely. Besides, I'd learned from hospital volunteer work (especially with paralyzed people) that sympathy is the worst thing you can give a handicapped person. They usually respond to treating them naturally or even with a bit of hostility. I felt the hostility was going to come out whether I wanted it to or not.

I'd walk off and leave Jerry staring. In a few minutes, he'd holler, "Mannie"—a name he hadn't called me since we were quite young and dating—"I need you."

I'd run up the stairs two at a time.

Still, he didn't receive my help with gratitude, I didn't think.

"Help me bathe." We started with his feet. He'd lift them into the sink, one at a time.

As I'd remove one foot from the sink Jerry often said, "You missed my heel."

I'd glare at him and stick the foot back down.

"The water's too hot now," he complained.

Then he said, "You didn't dry in between my toes."

"Footwashing is a spiritual thing. They do it in a lot of churches.

You're supposed to receive this lovingly. Jesus even did it for the disciples," I said.

"I'll bet He dried in between their toes," Jerry mumbled.

As I'd wash his good, left arm and back, he had more suggestions to offer. I'd dry him with unnecessary roughness, and he'd glare at me. At that point I could have marched away angrily and thrown the towel on his head. One thing saved us. It was the thing that I'd loved about Jerry the first time we dated, long before I ever thought about loving him.

His humor.

I'd started out of the bathroom fuming, when he called, "Hey, nurse. You forgot the *left* guard."

I came back and my face broke into a smile. Then I laughed out loud. Picking up the can of Right Guard, I sprayed.

"Not in one spot, dummy, all around."

With that I sprayed him all over and he ran out of the bathroom.

"You sure they let you work in hospitals?"

It was time to get his pants on. He only had two pairs that he liked to wear around the house. "Which pair do you think I should wear?"

I shrugged my shoulders and decided on the brown ones. I'm left-handed so I held out the left leg first.

"Other leg."

"What difference does it make?"

"I want the other leg first!"

I held the right leg up—*way up* above his waist.

"Could you lower it?"

I lowered it almost to the floor and he glared at me.

I got tickled again and fell on the floor laughing. Jerry stood waiting quite composed. I'd skip belt loops when I put his belt on, and he made me do it over.

I wanted to put on one sock and one shoe, then go to the other foot.

He wanted both socks on first. And I forgot to straighten the toes. I tied his shoes too tight.

Before we put on his shirt, he said, "I want to wear a T-shirt."

"Well, you can't."

"The strap on my cast hurts my middle."

I glared at him.

"Fix me a T-shirt."

I got the scissors and cut off the bottom four inches of a T-shirt, and with quite a bit of coaxing from me, he finally agreed to step into it. He grinned happily and said, "That feels good."

When we went to the doctor, he asked me quickly, "What's that white thing around Jerry's waist?"

"His T-shirt," I answered matter-of-factly.

The doctor nodded and grunted, "Good idea."

It had been over a week since the accident, and a friend and I were talking. I told her how things were going and how Jerry didn't seem to like the way I did things for him—"and I have to do *every-thing* for him," I added.

She laughed and said, "Marion, don't you remember how you've been wanting to do little things for Jerry and spend time with him and feel needed?"

A light seemed to go on in my head and I whispered, "Of course."

My whole attitude about Jerry changed right that moment. I don't believe God causes accidents or pain, and I don't want to get into theology—I don't know enough about it—but I remembered that as soon as Jerry came home from the hospital we all prayed for his healing and we are receiving it (without surgery). But the Lord has a unique way of using bad things to His glory, and I believe this was one of those times.

I realized that I had Jerry all to myself each day. *He needed me.* Why, he had started doing one of the things that I'd wanted for so long—hanging around the kitchen, watching me do the dishes. Making small talk.

We often ate breakfast out together, *alone.*

Anytime during the day I could go sit by him.

And in spite of his injury, we were laughing together again, like we had on dates twenty-three years ago. There were deeper moments, too, when we silently held each other closely—well, as closely as we could. We'd separate laughing about the cast that prevented us from getting too close.

Another bonus came out of the accident. For years I'd listened to Christian tapes by ministers that really had something exciting to say. I'd tried to entice Jerry or anyone in my family to listen with me, but they always ran the other way, asking, "Please, turn that thing down."

Several people brought Jerry some Christian tapes. He smiled and was most gracious. After they left, before they were even out of the driveway, I'd offer, "Want me to play the tape?"

"No," he'd bellow. "Why do people bring me tapes?"

I know if I hadn't been so pushy he probably would have learned to enjoy them long ago, but I'd really overdone it.

"I have no idea," I answered. "Why don't you throw them back at them, or simply stomp them on the floor in front of the people?"

"I will," he said.

"Good," I replied.

Several days later the phone rang, and Jerry, who almost never answers it, just looked at it. I was cooking and said, "Get it, will you?"

He did and I heard him say, "Sure, I'd love them. We'll be home, and thank you."

The smile left his face as he hung up and he said, "Dianne is coming over with some stuff." He said it without enthusiasm. I knew Dianne had loads of good tapes, and I sort of hoped.

She arrived in a little while with our lunch and *two tapes*. She smiled radiantly and explained, "I've brought physical food and spiritual food. That's what the Lord told me to do." She seemed as excited as a child on Christmas morning about her mission. She never stopped smiling.

Jerry thanked her profusely. I glanced at the tapes and almost danced a jig right there in the kitchen. They were by one of my favorite Bible teachers.

"Oh," she added, "these are for you to keep, Jerry. Don't send them back. I recorded them for you from my tapes. See, they have your name on them."

Jerry bent to look. After Dianne left, we ate the food in silence. I didn't mention the tapes. Since he hadn't thrown them at Dianne, I thought he just might throw them at me. After lunch Jerry went upstairs. His hand had been swelling a lot, and the only thing that relieved it was to lie in the hospital bed for several hours. He'd already told me that there was nothing on television but garbage. I rejoiced silently. I'd been telling him that for two years.

As I folded clothes, I thought I heard someone talking. I tiptoed up the steps and listened for a moment. Jerry was listening to the tapes! I ran back downstairs and said right out loud, "Hallelujah." He listened for almost two hours. Then he called, "Mannie, you've got to come hear these tapes. They are really something. Come listen."

We listened to them, and he played them later over and over. He even played them for company.

Another blessing during his recuperation was that we started back having family devotionals. It was the boys who gathered us together each evening, once Jerry had said that he wanted us to resume our devotional time together. We seemed to have time now for many things that used to be crowded out of our schedules. In fact, Jerry's accident had slowed down our entire life-style. We are almost like a music box that needs winding. Only I don't want us to be wound up tight again. I like the new pace.

And so we read the Bible and prayed together almost every evening. Always our prayers were of thanksgiving that the Lord was healing Jerry's arm without surgery and that it was healing good and strong. We prayed for other personal needs, too.

One evening we read from the Bible that a sparrow can't fall to the ground without God knowing about it. We all looked at each other and smiled reassuringly. Then, surely a daddy and husband can't fall from a ladder either, without the Lord seeing and knowing and having things under control. We felt the Presence of the Lord in a special way that night.

Jerry and I were overwhelmed at the kind things people did for us. Two men came over and cleaned up the tree limbs in the back. Fruit, candy, books, phone calls, visits, cards came daily. People assured Jerry of their prayers. I don't think I've ever seen him so grateful.

Gradually he learned to lean on the children and me more comfortably. I learned how to bathe his feet and dry in between the toes.

I stopped begging him to talk to me. Sometimes we just sat before the fire and looked at the flames and contentment rose up inside me. There was no reason to say anything. One cold, windy morning, we both went to sleep on the sofa holding hands with our collie lying across both of us. It was delicious.

I declined to go many places and gave up responsibilities so that I could stay at home with Jerry. However, I'd lined up several speaking engagements before he was hurt, and I felt I had to keep those. Jerry encouraged me to. On the Monday after he'd broken his arm, I had to go way across town. I was to leave at nine and wouldn't be back until nearly three. It seemed strange for me to be leaving Jerry. He was always leaving me; going to work, to meetings, out of town. It was horrible some days when the boys were babies and the rain was falling and I knew loneliness and depression were waiting to overtake me. Sometimes I'd cry watching him dress.

On that rainy Monday, he watched me dress and then sat in the living room with me waiting for my ride. I felt gloom in the house. "It'll be a long day," he said softly. Right then I wanted so much not to go, but I knew I had to. As I drove off, he stood at the window and waved good-bye.

I could hardly wait to get back to him.

Despite our "feuds" about my helping him to his satisfaction, I saw my husband in a marvelous new light. It was the little things I noticed. Like how he didn't complain—not really. He joked about his arm. People loved to visit with him. Laughter burst forth quickly from Jerry and the visitors. He never mentioned that the hospital bed was too short and that he had to sleep with his feet pushing against the end to keep from sliding down in the bed. He didn't lie around bed all day, but got up and got dressed. He even whistled when he shaved. He smiled a lot and helped the children with a new patience with their homework. He listened to the boys intently. He encouraged Jeremy in some project he was building—a volcano, of all things. He went over Jon's school papers in detail with him.

When the doctor had to manipulate his arm twice and put two other casts on it, I saw Jerry flinch, but he didn't complain. And when the doctor was over two hours late one day for an office visit because of emergency surgery, Jerry waited patiently while I fumed.

When the doctor had Jerry fitted for an arm brace, which held his arm out at an eighty-degree angle, it was an experience for both of us. First of all, I had to drive him downtown. (I don't drive downtown.) He was giving me directions but had forgotten his glasses. His arm was highly sensitive since there wasn't any protection of any kind on it, and he told me about each bump I hit.

He was measured and fitted for the brace, but the full impact of what it would be like didn't hit us until we went back, three days later, to have it put on. When the men brought it into the examining room to strap it on, a look crossed Jerry's face that I haven't seen often. Once I saw it when Jeremy almost died as a baby. Again I saw it when I told him I was writing a book about *us* (*Out of My Bondage*). And the latest time had been when Julie told us she was getting married. Jerry's only comment when he saw the brace had been, "It looks like something you put on a horse." But his face said much more. While we waited in the examining room for them to make more adjustments on the brace, depression entered the room, like a deadly gas seeping under the door. My words of encouragement were useless. I stepped outside for a moment to check on our bill, and the waiting room was almost full. Many of the patients were children. Two of them were in body braces. One little black girl, who was unbelievably thin and twisted, sat captured in her brace. Her parents looked straight ahead. Her head was bent. She had pigtails with bright red ribbon on them. When she breathed, it sounded like someone in an iron lung. I looked at her and felt tears rising up inside me. Just then she looked at me and smiled.

I smiled back. In a few minutes they took her into a room and shut the door and I heard her screams. When I went back into Jerry's room, I told him about the little girl. He listened, nodding his head. He sat up straighter, and we started making normal conversation again. The depression was chased out of the room.

Driving home, we got tickled. Jerry's arm was up in a waving position, and people waved at us. Jerry smiled and waved back.

Getting into bed and to sleep, however, wasn't a smiling matter. The brace was extremely uncomfortable. It put a terrible strain on his shoulder. When we called the brace people to be sure it was fitted properly, we were told that it usually takes patients seven to ten days to learn to sleep with it. The man added, "Some people take them off in desperation. I hope you won't do that."

I tried every way I could think of to get Jerry comfortable. But sleeping with your arm up in the air takes some getting used to. For the first time since the break, Jerry's face was filled with pain. We moved down to the den, and I tried to make him comfortable in a reclining chair. Then I couldn't leave him down there alone, so I made a bed on the sofa. In about an hour his hand was asleep and we trudged back upstairs to try to find a comfortable position for him in the hospital bed.

Several more times, I got up to make adjustments. He didn't know what to tell me to do, so often we just stared at each other in the moonlight.

After the fourth attempt to get him comfortable, I went back to bed and prayed simply, "Help, Lord. Help. We can't do it. Please, help us." I thought about how Jesus couldn't move at all on the cross and of the agony of being unable to change positions.

In a few minutes, I listened. Jerry's breathing told me that he was asleep! I thanked the Lord and promptly went to sleep. Jerry slept all night. He had planned to attend a deacon's retreat with our church the next morning. I hadn't encouraged him, but he wanted to do it. One of the deacons was picking him up. He would be gone all day.

I got up at six thirty to help him dress. He didn't seem to need much help. He was whistling while he shaved. At breakfast—a glass of milk and a sweet roll—he thanked the Lord for the food, for the brace, for the good night's sleep . . . and for me.

His ride came by, and he left smiling. Even that early in the morning I smiled too. I smiled long after he was gone.

I had finally figured out how to get a complete T-shirt on him, and he was greatly pleased with that. He kept telling me how good it felt. I felt like Jerry's helpmeet, in every sense of the word. I felt needed.

Through the accident, there were obvious changes in all of us. Jennifer, who'd been sulky and unwilling to help me unless I made her, began to smile. We had conversations again. One night she insisted on making supper. I had to speak at a meeting that night and had a headache. She cleaned up the kitchen beautifully.

Jeremy told me, "Mama, I know you have a lot to do now; I picked up the bathroom even though it was Jon's mess, and I'm going to bring the dirty clothes down to the washroom before you ask me to."

Jon brought in wood for the fire without being asked to. One day I told him to write a two-page essay for something he'd done wrong. Instead of protesting or begging for a one-page essay, he said, "Okay." In fifteen minutes—record time—he handed me the best essay he'd ever written. There were only two small errors and the handwriting was beautiful. So was the message. I gave Jon his first A plus. Here's the essay:

> When you forgive somebody you mean that what they did is all right. When you do something wrong you should ask God to forgive you. But He won't forgive you unless you ask Him in your heart. The Bible says you should forgive someone who has done wrong 490 times. That's seven times seventy. When they nailed Jesus to the cross and spit on Him and called names, He said, forgive them, Father, for they know not what they do. Now if Jesus can do that then surely you can forgive somebody when they do something to bother you.
> Forgiveness is a sign of kindness and love. When you ask God to forgive you, you must forget completely about it.
> When you sin, you must always ask for forgiveness because if you don't you will be asked in heaven why you didn't.
> When you forgive somebody do it because you love them, not just to be good.
> So the next time you forgive somebody, remember why you're doing it.
> And always forgive others.

I came to understand that essay in a clearer light very soon. For years Jon has had a problem with admitting anything is his fault. It's always someone else's fault. He almost can't admit anything is his fault. I saw Jerry, quite simply, bring about a sort of miracle in Jon's life. The night of the accident, we were all finally in bed and I didn't know it but Jon slipped into Jennifer's room and told her something. She told me the next morning in hushed tones: "Mama, Jon told me the accident was all his fault." She explained what Jon had told her. He'd said, "Jennifer, when Daddy was up on the ladder, I pulled at a limb on the ground. It wouldn't come completely off the tree, so I let it go. It flipped and hit the ladder."

When Jennifer told me that, I remembered how quiet Jon had been when he came into the house with his daddy. He'd looked pale, too, but I hadn't had time to spend with him. I was trying to figure out what was wrong with Jerry.

I remembered too that while Jerry and Ricky were at the emergency room, I'd been looking out the kitchen window and watched Jon moving about in the back yard—right where the accident happened. He seemed to be almost re-enacting something, or playing, I wasn't sure which. But he looked so thoughtful. He grabbed at a limb, walked with it, still connnected to the tree by the bark, and then let it go. It snapped back like a slingshot. I hadn't thought anything about it at the time. Jerry had told me that he asked Jon if he saw anything move on the ground. Jerry had been so sure that the ladder had been knocked out from under him.

"No, sir," Jon had said.

Jon had lied on top of moving the limb as he tried to help.

He'd picked Jennifer to share his heavy burden of guilt and terror with.

The next morning I told Jerry what had happened. He nodded his head and said, "I knew something hit that ladder with a force." Then a look of gentleness came in his eyes—one like I've seldom seen.

At breakfast Jon and Jerry and I were the only ones left at the table. Jon seemed to be staring at his daddy's arm. He was very quiet, which is highly unusual for Jon. He talks nonstop.

Jerry began, "Jon, Jennifer told us what you told her last night, son. She had to."

Jon looked almost expressionless and sat perfectly still awaiting whatever was to come.

Jerry continued, "Son, you must not for one second blame yourself. We were working together. You were my helper, and you're good help. You're a good worker. I needed you. It wasn't your fault, not one bit. Don't you ever believe it was. I'm going to be fine, and we're going to cut down more limbs together, okay?"

Jon was silent for a moment. Then he answered, "Okay." He slid out of his chair and walked past Jerry's chair and stopped and leaned against his father's shoulder for a moment. Then he walked on out the door.

Jerry and I finished our coffee slowly, quietly. I'd gotten a replacement for my Sunday school class. I was going to stay at home with Jerry that day. Jennifer took the boys to Sunday school and church. I had a feeling that Jon had learned more in the last few minutes than he would at the services, but I sent him anyway.

All of us have learned during Jerry's recuperation—even the cat. Our new cat is rough and doesn't let you love him easily. He's suspicious and keeps his distance except on rare occasions.

Jerry had been complaining, "Mannie, this cat rubs up against my legs all the time and gets hair on my pants. Why does he have to lean on *me?*"

"He's learning to love," I replied.

Jerry didn't complain about the cat leaning on him anymore, and the cat promptly attached himself to Jerry. He followed him as closely as Jon.

Seems like the verb "to lean" is constantly being practiced around our house since Jerry got hurt. I lean, you lean, he leans; we lean, you lean, they lean.

We all seem to be learning to lean on each other and on the One with the everlasting arms Who welcomes leaners.

# THE JOY OF LEANING

The day started out great. I awoke anticipating an evening out with my husband and our new friends, Gina and O. J. Greene. Even though we'd just met the Greenes, our spirits seemed to have been quickened by the Holy Spirit so that it was as though we'd been friends since childhood. "Ah," I thought, still lying in bed for a few luxurious moments, "today isn't too crowded. Nothing special planned. Don't have to do a lot of driving, no meetings. I'll just spend the day looking forward to tonight when the four of us will eat somewhere really nice. We can take our time and talk."

The morning went well. I was way ahead of schedule. In the afternoon I decided on the spur of the moment to take the paint off a small, very old table. I'd meant to do it for years. Carefully I applied the paint remover. But I didn't read the directions. I abhor directions of any kind. I waited a few minutes and proceeded to rub the paint off. Most of it didn't come off. The paint that did come off sat like hard, wrinkled balls stuck to the table. I squirted the hose on the mess and the cold water seemed to "freeze" the peeling paint even harder.

I'd spilled some of the remover on the patio and on myself. The remover began burning my hands. I noticed the directions recommended gloves. There was also something about waiting quite a while before trying to remove the paint remover. "Well, little table, you aren't going to ruin my evening. I'll forget about you for today." But thoughts of the half-stripped table remained stubbornly in my mind. I loved that table.

I came into the kitchen. I'd left it spotless and knew I'd feel better there. My fifteen-year-old daughter was making a cake—without my permission. Flour and eggs covered the counter tops. Some had spilled onto the floor. "Mama, please take me to the store to get some cocoa. We don't have any. I have to take this cake to a bake sale at school tomorrow. I promised."

"Stay cool," I told myself. "Don't let this ruin your day or your beautiful evening." "Okay," I managed, glancing at the messy kitchen, "but you clean this up when we get home."

"I will. Let me take my cakes out of the oven before we go. They're ready." She lifted the two layers out and, somehow, as if in slow motion, turned one upside down in midair. Out of the corner of her eyes she quickly looked at me. The cake landed in the middle of the floor. Jennifer leaned over and lifted the pan off. "It didn't stick." She tried to smile.

Jeremy came through the door and said, "Hey, great, now I can eat some of it." He sat on the floor and began eating the broken cake. The cat came to join him.

"Mama, I'm sorry," Jennifer said softly.

I thought: "My day's not going so good after all, but I won't blow it. I mustn't scream. That won't help." But that's what I felt like doing.

"Let's go get the cocoa, Jen. I need to get some paint remover or something to get this stuff off my hands." The remover had turned my skin a bright red on three of my fingers. "You can clean up the cake when we get back." Jennifer and Jeremy and I got into the car and started for the store. I let her off at a grocery store and I went on to a hardware store across the street to get something to try to get my hand back to normal. After I made my purchase, I hurriedly backed out the car. Someone screamed loud and long. Glancing into the rear-view mirror, I saw a little lady right behind me. She seemed to have come from nowhere. "You almost ran over me," she said hoarsely, leaning against my car. She wasn't even five feet tall.

"Are you all right?" I asked. "Oh, I'm so sorry." My heart was pounding.

"Yes, I seem to be."

A wave of nausea went through me when I thought of what had almost happened. "The muscles in the back of my neck are getting stiff," I thought. "I don't want the tension that I feel coming."

I picked up Jennifer and Jeremy and we started home. Jen sat in the front with me, and Jeremy in the back seat. Suddenly Jennifer looked backward and screamed, "Jer-eee-meee!"

Panic shot through me, but for some reason I didn't stop the car. I continued around the curve I was driving on and then glanced back in the rear-view mirror. I saw the door closing and Jeremy "coming back" into the car.

"Mama," Jennifer screamed, "he fell out. The door came open and he went out and kept holding on. Then the door shut again and he came back in. Oh, Mama, he was hanging out in the street!"

"Lock the door, Jen," I said almost mechanically, still driving. I hadn't stopped the car but had slowed down. We were in traffic. I continued home slowly, gripping the wheel. My neck muscles were now very tight.

At home we pulled into the driveway and piled out of the car. From down the street came the complaints of a neighbor. Jon had ridden his bike through her yard. He knew better. I was sorry but couldn't seem to get the words out. I told Jon to get off his bike and ignored his loud protests.

Inside Jennifer cleaned up the cake, and outside I tried to get the red stuff off my hands. It wouldn't come off. I went into the kitchen to get a towel and saw that Jennifer was mixing the icing without cooking it. ("Just like me," I thought. "She doesn't read directions.") "You have to let the icing come to a boil, Jennifer." I took the aluminum mixing bowl and put it on the stove's eye. "Won't take but a jiffy," I explained.

When I removed the mixing bowl, I automatically slid my hand under it since there wasn't a handle. I wasn't used to a mixing bowl's being hot.

Indescribable pain shot through my fingers, hand, and seemed to travel right into my brain. For a few seconds, my fingers stuck to the bottom of the bowl. Maybe the paint remover and kerosene added severity to the burn. I knew instantly that I'd really messed up my fingers.

I ran for ice and quickly stuck my three fingers into a bowl of ice water. Relief was instant and delicious. Jennifer watched in seeming horror. "Don't scream," I told myself. "It won't help."

*What's going to happen next?*

What happened was that when I tried to remove my hand from the bowl of ice water, even for a second, I had to return it immediately. And my fingers were still bright red from the paint remover. The clock ticked away. I should have already started dressing for our big evening out. A dull headache had begun and intensified quickly.

While Jennifer iced her one-layer cake, I went upstairs, undressed, and was about to step into the tub (still holding my bowl of ice water) when I heard, "Mama, I forgot to tell you that the Spanish class is eating out at a Spanish restaurant tonight. Please take me to school now or they'll leave me. I almost forgot with all that's happened."

I thought helplessly, this is unreal. With my hand still in the ice water, I clumsily redressed and drove Jennifer to the school with one hand. As I let her out, she said, "I feel sick at my stomach from eating so much icing. What if I throw up?"

I couldn't muster up any sympathy. "You'll be fine."

Back at home the phone was ringing when I entered the kitchen. I answered it and held it under my chin, while I got out more ice cubes for my bowl of water. Looking out the window at my table I heard over the phone, "Hi, Marion. You busy? I've had a terrible day and need to talk to someone about a problem."

A problem! What would it be like to have only one problem? My eyes filled with tears. I blinked them away, laid my aching head against the cool window, and listened.

Finally, back in the bathtub with my hand in ice water, a thought came to me: *"Don't go tonight. Your day has been too bad. Stay home. You're all tense and can't have a good time. What if something else happens?"*

I knew who the thoughts were from, but I listened anyway. I didn't even feel like praying. Dressing with one hand is next to impossible when you're used to two. Buttons and zippers made me want to scream like Tarzan.

Just then I heard Julie driving in from work, which meant it must be six o'clock. I'd forgotten to take the boys to ball practice!

"Julie," I called from the upstairs window, "please take the boys to practice for me. They're already late." I could tell from her expression that she didn't want to, but she said, "Okay, Mama."

"Hurry, boys," she urged. They moved slowly and crawled into the car with all their ball equipment.

Julie is an excellent driver. She has more confidence than I do and has never had any kind of a mishap. But that day she backed into our car in the driveway. Her father arrived home in his car pool just in time to witness the impact.

The pesky inner voice urged again, "*Stay home tonight.*"

Julie smiled weakly at her father and drove off with the boys.

I ran downstairs to greet Jerry and his expression revealed instantly to me that he'd had a rough day, even though he didn't say it. As we walked into the house together, he picked up my tenseness and asked sharply, "Why is your hand in that bowl?"

"I burned it."

I lifted my hand up for him to see. "Why is it red?"

"That's paint."

I was about to explain about the table when he looked out in the back yard and asked, "Why is the little table ruined and paint all over the patio?"

"I can fix it and get the paint up." I went upstairs mechanically to finish dressing.

My husband bellowed, "What happened to this cake? Why is it so little?"

Anger exploded in me, and I started back down the steps to tell him off. I rushed down the steps with what I was about to say already forming in my mind. I caught the pocket of my dress on the banister and ripped it slightly. It was the green dress Cora had sold me. The rip didn't seem so slight to me. It was as though a mountain had fallen on top of me. I couldn't take anything else. It seemed that something deep inside me had ripped too.

Jerry had gone to dress without waiting for an answer to his latest question. I stood on the steps and whispered, "Dear Lord, what's happening? What's wrong? I can't take this. I just can't take any more."

The gentle answer came quickly: "*Lean on me.*"

"Oh, Lord! Was I going on my own again?"

"*Yes, you have this stubborn streak that keeps appearing. You forget to lean.*"

I sighed physically and spiritually and eased back into leaning once more. I felt like a weary child once again in the arms of a caring parent.

Now that I was leaning, I could be completely honest. "Lord, I've lost my joy about tonight."

"*Count it all joy.*"

"All joy! Today?"

"*All joy. Yes, today.*"

"Today's joy!"

"*Yes.*"

I got my Bible and hunted for the familiar passage. I had to look for a few minutes but located it in James 1:2. I read from the New American Standard Bible. "Consider it all joy when you encounter various trials, knowing that your faith produces endurance."

"*Consider it all joy.*"

"All right, Lord, I'll count it joy because Your Word says to—not because I feel like it."

I began to list my "joys" for the day in my mind:

1. I didn't kill or injure that little lady.
2. Jeremy wasn't killed or hurt.
3. I burned my right hand and I'm left-handed.
4. Ice stops this pain. Thank You for ice.
5. Jennifer still has half a cake. It might be just what someone can afford at the bake sale.
6. As of this moment, I'm going to trust You to show me how to fix my table. I won't believe it's ruined.
7. Julie didn't even dent the car.
8. If I hold my arm down a bit, the torn pocket on my dress doesn't show.

I was about to come up with number nine when the doorbell interrupted my counting. I knew it was the Greenes. Holding my arm over the pocket of my dress, with my hand resting in the bowl of ice water, I opened the door and said, "Hi." My headache and tense muscles were gone. The joy was back! I felt a smile begin deep inside me and reach my face.

Gina and O.J. came in, and Gina asked with concern, "What happened to your hand?"

"It's burned, but it's going to be okay. Hope you don't mind if I take my ice water with us."

"Of course not," they said in unison.

"It's really been a day, Gina, except that I'm counting it all joy and leaning on Jesus."

She clapped her hands together silently and said, "Well, praise the Lord!" Jerry came down the steps, smiling, and greeted the Greenes. His eyes met mine for a brief instant, and we communicated without words. My joy increased.

The icy water felt wonderful to my fingers as the four of us drove to the restaurant. I had no guarantee that tonight or tomorrow would be any smoother than today. Nevertheless I decided to expect the best.

Driving down the expressway, I became aware of the faces of people in passing cars. Some were coming home from work—others going out for the evening. Almost no one smiled. Most people appeared grim. Oh, how I suddenly wanted them to know happiness and joy. I wanted to stop traffic and tell the sad-looking people that happiness doesn't have to depend on circumstances.

But I couldn't do that. I had to do something so I began humming the tune of "Learning to Lean" and thinking about the simple words that explain the secret of joyful living through learning to lean on Jesus.